WILL
POWER

The Call to Rise Above

PATRICIA W. GOINGS

First Printing, 2018

Will Power: The Call to Rise Above
ISBN: 978-0-692-91719-0
E-book ISBN: 978-0-692-91720-6
Copyright © 2018 by Patricia W. Goings

ACKNOWLEDGEMENTS

With love and fond memories, this book is dedicated to my mother, grandparents, and godmother—who always provided love, affection, and biblical instructions. To my wonderful sons, Tyrone, Michael, and Maurice, thank you for always encouraging me to move forward no matter how hard the pain.

To Pastor Jeannette Harley, Elder Dr. Edward McNeil, and Dr. Calvin L. Lewis, who continue to believe in my dreams and help me to grow in Christ, always providing prayer, guidance, and prophecy.

To my wonderful editor, Witness Publishing Group, thank you for traveling on this journey with me. It has been an amazing opportunity to work with you, and I am truly looking forward to additional published works with you in the years to come.

To the many others who supported me, I thank you for your patience and support. Most of all, I thank God, who made this book possible from conception all the way to reality. I am truly thankful You have chosen me to empower others and inspire them to know that in Christ Jesus all things are possible.

CONTENTS

INTRODUCTION

I was cast upon thee from the womb; Thou art my
God from my mother's belly.

PSALM 22:10

By building our trust and faith in God, we receive the
everlasting strength to prevail. We become victorious survivors over the storms of life. Power, strength,
and courage are all meaningful mechanisms that contrib-
ute to our existence and destiny. Collaboratively, these
are just a few characteristics which formulate who we are
and who we will become.

Our faith and belief must be like the strength of an
eagle. The eagle is a regal bird, and at the approach of a
storm, the eagle has the wherewithal to not get tossed or
disoriented. The eagle knows how to position its wings in

order to ride the storm and let the storm winds elevate it to a higher altitude. Eagles do not escape storms. They merely utilize storms for their advantage by using the storm to rise to another level. Much like the eagle, we as human beings inevitably face storms in our existence here on earth. Be that as it may, it is important that we be equipped to handle these tumults when they arise. How do we equip ourselves? It is by having a personal relationship with Jesus Christ and by walking in faith, hope, and God's love. As we journey through life, it is imperative that we become engaged in a lasting relationship with the Lord Jesus Christ—one which entails confessing our faults, repenting of our sins, being water baptized in the name of Jesus, and receiving the gift of the Holy Spirit. Stretching our arms on the wings of faith, hope, and God's love gives us the will power to soar above the storm.

I have now arrived at a point and time in my life where I clearly understand how God has a divine will and plan for my life. Understanding the story of Eve—the first female and first woman created by God—has given me strength, grace, and courage for my life's journey. Imagine being born, created, and formed from the rib of a man. Eve set the path that brought on the changes that have lasted throughout generations until this very day. Her ability to distract Adam and cause him to follow her into deceitfulness ushered bitterness and disobedience into the world. Yet, Adam had been forewarned by God, as he was told not to eat of the forbidden fruit. God, even until this day, gives each one of us a choice; that's the pure love of our heavenly Father.

Eve left behind a story that impacts our life one day at a time, day after day, and year after year. I have learned to stand up for the things I believe in and the things that are unquestionably pleasing to God. God created each woman with the gift of life, love, and hope. Let us walk and journey on, living for God in unity, truth, and spirituality. We were created in God's image to be princesses full of love and compassion. Additionally, we are charged to be faithful to our wonderful, heavenly Father. He is the Lord of lords and King of kings, and He reigns forever.

My story consists of life-learning lessons, many of which represent multiple stages and periods of development. Some of these lessons were very challenging, and some have been very rewarding. Despite the nature of the lessons we experience, one's development increases both in a physical and mental facet. Life is a journey in which one must and will travel to different schools and places and also experience many types of trials; yet we must find joy through it all. My life has been a true story of survival, struggles, and salvation and is only written to help others become empowered and encouraged through God's grace.

I have often heard people talk about the will to live or about having the will to fight. It is during the latter stages of adulthood that I became more and more determined to live and fight for the life God has given me. Life is wonderful. Life is beautiful. Life is full of God's glory. God created the heavens, the earth, and everything that allows us to exist. It is because of Him that we exist. At some point in your life, as things sometimes start to look bleak or appear to be torn upside down, you may ask the question: "Am I in a mess?" Sometimes you may even venture to question whether life is really good or not. Oh yes! Life is good. It is a gift from God. It is predestined by God and is full of God's promises and worth all of the turmoil we will ever experience.

As I think about what Jesus went through, I cannot even begin to see myself walking in His shoes. But since we have nothing to lose, why not fight with all we can and trust in the King that gives us the strength, power, and promise that we can do all things if we believe?

Think about your life and reflect on the good as well as the things that made you disheartened. As children of the King, the Highest, and the Lord of lords, we are blessed through it all. We have a Father like none other, seated on the throne where He reigns as the true, living Lord. He is the Alpha and Omega, the One who can and will bring us over every mountain. Throughout our lives, we have to climb many hills, and we still have the tendency to complain even after we consider what Jesus went through. What really matters at the end of our travailing is that we have held on to our faith and trust in the Lord to bring us to the top of the mountain.

It is inevitable that life will present situations and circumstances that will cause us to wonder. I believe that it is during these times that our faith is being built, our trust is being tested, and our total being becomes submitted to the Lord for His glory. Can we forget how God brings us through the deepest valley? No, we can never forget the wonders of the Lord. Our God performs wonders every day. The fact that we are alive, seeing the dawn, and awakened to each new day the Lord has made, speaks volumes to having to climb over any mountain. At this point in your life's journey you may be asking yourself the question, "How many more mountains, trials, and situations will I have to face?" Only God knows the answer, yet I would dare ask Him. But I do believe and guarantee that He will see you through. When it comes right down to it, I trust Him; I love Him and adore Him more than anything. God has never left me standing or in a situation that He was not willing to help me get through. Thus, it is significant that we look to Him in our time of trouble, seeking and having the will power to answer His call to rise above.

God is ever so faithful to His children and those that believe in Him. God can speak to the wind and the rain (troubles of life) and command them to obey His desire for our lives. I have often found myself somewhat down during the rain, but as life evolves and I age spiritually and naturally, I have come to realize the beauty of the rain. I arrived at a place when I was pushed, pushed, and pushed. I felt all alone and had been tossed aside by the very ones I trusted. But through it all, advocating and cheering me on was the precious love, grace, and mercy that comes from above, from the Vine—our heavenly Father who perpetually and continuously watches over us. Praise His name, for He is marvelous; He is wonderful, great, and mighty. When the storms of life drive us to the point of despair, we can still count on and look to God, our refuge, to see us T.H.R.O.U.G.H.

RIDING THROUGH THE STORM

He maketh the storm a calm, so that the waves thereof
are still.

PSALM 107:29

It is amazing how we often refer to the rain in casual
sentiment. It is also interesting to me how others not
only view the significance of the rain, but how they define the rain. For many, the rain is simply just a
downpour falling from the sky. Others may see it is as an
event from heaven, or some may even say nothing at all
about the rain. As a child, the worst of many sayings was
that the rain meant the devil was beating his wife. Ha ha,
wrong thought. God's work (His creation) surely has no
evil in it.

During my younger years, rain simply meant water falling from the sky. I was taught at an early age that rain was symbolic of God showering down blessings. On most rainy days, sitting on the porch and playing the usual games was not permissible nor could the neighborhood children hop across the banisters adjacent to each house. As I often sat in the window and watched the rain fall, the busy action in the streets, and the passing cars blow their horns, little did I know that life was revealing who I was and who I would become. I was about to embrace and endure days that one would only read about or hopefully tell as an inspirational story. There was no way I ever fathomed that this would be my story and others would read about it. Neither did I ever imagine that I would soon have to deal with many losses, hurt, hardships, and pain. At this time, I had no idea that any of this was my story, time of transition, or destiny calling me through it all.

I had a loving family and lots of friends; and of course I was known as and referred to as the "spoiled child" by many family members and those closest to my family. I was considered spoiled because of the love that I received and because toys and clothes were always made available to me at my request. As a child, I was blessed to receive gifts that every child coveted. Be it birthdays, Christmas, or family gatherings, I always received something. I was the only girl in the family for almost thirty years, so I would say that I wore the title of "spoiled" very well.

Having been spoiled so much left an indelible portrait of my childhood in my mind. Reflecting now over my childhood, I remember the cold wintry days growing up in Philadelphia, when the crystal white snow appeared to fall endlessly from the sky. At times, visibility was a virtual impossibility; and you could hardly see anything but the snow. Although the visibility during the snow storms was difficult, this still did not prevent people from trying to drive through the snow-covered streets. On the other hand, there were a number of people who stood waiting on street corners for the bus or trolley cars to take them to work or to shop. You would always see people everywhere looking out of the windows of the cars, buses, or passing trains—waving while others stood waiting for the next bus or train to arrive. Yet, the delays did not really seem to matter to me at times, and many others did not appear to be troubled by the weather. It was wintertime nonetheless, and I wondered at times how many people really knew it was God's divine plan for the season. The crystal white snow—whiter than any other shade of white known to man—was a perfect picture to see falling from the sky. I saw it as God's love descending upon mankind, although some may say the snowy season is cold and not their favorite time of the year; yet the change in seasons has meaning in its own way. Noticeably, I was able to observe a few people that did not appear to be troubled by the weather and managed to smile despite the snow. People could be seen making their way to the bus stop or getting in their cars after scraping the ice and snow from the hood and windows.

I remember laughing and hearing the loud voices and laughter of the neighborhood children as we ran up and down the sidewalks, playing in the snow. We often had snowball fights, and we enjoyed watching each other ride sleds with our neighbors. Building snowmen from the mounds of snow piled up in front of our houses was a ton of fun, but we also relished the idea of just being outdoors and having fun playing with each other.

At this time in life, we did not know any heartaches or pain; but little did I know that it was coming my way soon and would devastate my family, entire neighborhood, and church family. It would also have a lingering effect on the rest of my life too.

The neighborhood children could always be seen wearing bright and colorful blue, green, and yellow scarves wrapped around them, accenting their matching hats, gloves, and long coats. For the most part, the bright-colored snow boots that we wore kept our feet warm; but our feet still got wet anyway from the constant jumping and running in the snow and slush. Neither I nor the other children seemed bothered by the freezing temperatures. The pretty white snow would just keep falling and falling, and it appeared brighter and brighter as we played in it. Yet, it really did not seem to bother anyone as it continued falling and turning to shining white crystallized ice deposits on the ground as the temperature got colder.

Footprints on the sidewalks varied in size from the wide range of passengers who trekked through the snow. For us children, following the footprints was a way of having fun as we ran and stepped in the snow—comparing the sizes of our footprints to those left behind by others.

During my early childhood, the changing of the seasons did not have as great of an impact on my life as it would in the years to come. As children, we surely were delighted on the snowy days because school was closed, the buses were hardly running, and cars could be seen stuck in the snow as they slid from side to side. It was common to see a car collide with another car due to black ice (ice not readily visible to the naked eye) on the streets. But as children, nothing seemed to matter; and everything outside of ourselves was insignificant because we were still maturing and God was busy at work developing and preparing us for our life's journey and destiny.

Now that I am an adult, I have grown to know the Lord; I have a loving relationship with Him, one that is so sweet and precious. Moreover, knowing the Lord God like never before makes my understanding and behavior more appreciative of whom I have become. It was early in my childhood that life truly presented many challenges, and I am sure they may have happened to many of you as well. For many people, they have endured more challenging times, events, and circumstances than I may have, and I am certain that some have gone through less challenging ones. Wherein, each of our childhood stories is our own individual history, collection of testimonies, and ways of life.

I was born and raised in West Philadelphia; I was the popular kid amongst the neighborhood children. I attended church regularly with my parents and was involved with numerous church auxiliaries. I sang in the junior choir, served as a junior usher, and also competed in the King and Queen contest, proudly winning against the three older contestants. The outcome of the contest was very upsetting to a few members of the church because I was the youngest contestant, and it was everyone's premonition that one of the older contestants would win. However, it was announced and received by most of the congregation that Miss Paddy was unreservedly the winner. In all of the excitement, I could hear the voices uttering congratulatory phrases: "Make us proud, Pooh," "Do your best, and God will do the rest." Because I was the youngest contestant, I was subjected to ridicule and the occasional rejection of others.

If there was a pageant going on, I was there and had to be in it. I loved the pretty laced dresses, matching shoes, and accessories I often wore to the many pageants I competed in. My parents, godparents, uncles, and aunt made sure that I had outfits for every occasion. There was never a limit on the outfits because at times it seemed like every family member was bringing me an outfit to wear. My mother was a seamstress by trade and would often make many of the dresses and outfits that I wore. Proudly, I went on to win many competitions throughout the years. I learned how to compete and work for the success of the competition. I always knew that if I did my best whatever was to come my way would be mine. I was taught and understood that to become successful it would require me to stay on task and most importantly, believe in myself and the one and only Creator of all mankind, our wonderful Redeemer. I always heard the name of Jesus, and I was taught many stories in Sunday school about this wonderful man. But, oh, how I would learn just how wonderful Jesus is and would be in my life.

As believers in Christ, we are victorious in addition to having hope, unconditional love, and the promise of eternal life. It is God's desire that we are victorious; and pleasing our heavenly Father has the greatest rewards.

As I went on competing in and winning many other activities and events over the years, my parents could be seen sitting among the audience, wearing big smiles upon their faces. I noticed the smiles on their faces and could sense the pleasure it brought them. At times even, during the competitions, it was not even about the winning. My parents celebrated just my being in the event or activity. God calls His children to please Him in all that they do and say.

> My son, hear the instruction of thy father, and forsake not the law of thy mother: For they shall be an ornament of grace unto thy head, and chains about thy neck.
>
> PROVERBS 1:8-9

God instructs us to be faithful, honest, loving, and obedient in all that we do. My parents always reminded me that Jesus loved me and they loved me as well. Likewise, I loved my parents so indescribably; love and happiness were the only things I knew. To receive chastisement for doing something I knew I should not have done meant that my parents and those closest to me loved me and wanted only the best for me. What a spoiled child I was; some even say now in my later years, "Paddy is spoiled." Laughingly, I disagree, and I can't even imagine how one can still have this conclusion about me today. Maybe it *is* true in many ways that I am oblivious to!

My mom and dad loved the Lord with all their hearts. They taught me to pray, be dedicated in my church service, and attend Sunday school and vacation Bible school. Church was a regular practice for my family. My mother, as many would say, sang like an angel. As she was heard singing in the church choir, her voice echoed through the congregation louder than most but still had the softest and sweetest harmony. My mom was unmistakably gifted and deemed to have a voice which many said sounded like the songstress Mahalia Jackson. This was especially noticeable when she would sing her version of "He's Got the Whole World in His Hands." My mom not only sang the song but believed it wholeheartedly.

For the Lord is the great God, the great King above all gods. In his hand are the depths of the earth, and the mountain peaks belong to Him. The sea is his, for he made it, and his hands formed the dry land.

PSALM 95:3-5 (NIV)

Yes, our God does have the entire world in His hands. As a child, I knew little or nothing of how God controlled the world, but I did know that God created the heavens and the earth. I knew that God was big and that nothing was bigger, greater, or mightier than He. As I often listened to my mother ministering through music, it was an indicator to me that something was unique.My dad was a prayer warrior. He also sang and was often heard singing the song "Leaning on the Everlasting Arms" every Sunday with much pride and love for the Lord. My dad always stood tall and upright as he sang his favorite song. Without a doubt, he surely did lean on the Lord. The church service was uplifting, as the congregation would join him in singing. The difficulties and many challenges that awaited my dad would become a test of faith for my dad. On the other hand, dad's faith would be a true illustration of his belief. The significance of my dad's favorite song would later have an impact on my life as well. Now, many years have passed, and I can still hear the words of the song ringing in my ears:

What a fellowship, what a joy divine,

Leaning on the everlasting arms;

What a blessedness, what a peace is mine,

Leaning on the everlasting arms.

Leaning, leaning, safe and secure from all alarms;

Leaning, leaning, and leaning on the everlasting arms.

O how sweet to walk in this pilgrim way,

Leaning on the everlasting arms;

O how bright the path grows from day to day,

Leaning on the everlasting arms.

What have I to dread, what have I to fear,

Leaning on the everlasting arms?

I have blessed peace with my Lord so near,

Leaning on the everlasting arms.

Leaning on the everlasting arms of Jesus

Of who is our hope, our peace, joy and happiness.

Truly, my parents did let their lights shine; they leaned and depended on Jesus to see them through every test, trial, and situation. Jesus was all they ever needed and wanted for most of their life. I remember my parents sharing food with the less fortunate ones in our neighborhood. My parents were always willing to take our neighbors' children with us to church on Sunday. Additionally, they faithfully supported the church at most events until my mom's health was challenged. My dad continued to attend church regularly while my mom lay in the hospital week after week for several months. He would even attend the evening services after his afternoon visits with my mother at the hospital. My dad never gave up hope. Though he was hurt and saddened by the unexpected and rapidly declining health of my mother, my dad pressed his way to service with his hat in his warm hands, holding my little hand tightly as he led the way.

Our family often had family celebrations for every holiday until my mother's health presented many difficulties. Despite the impediment to my family being able to continue in many of our traditions, it was obvious that God was still at work. God was working through my parents in every circumstance that presented a challenge to them, even as the challenges occurred almost daily. However, both of my parents held on to their faith and trust in the Lord, never showing any signs of grief or despair. Knowing and having the assurance that Jesus is the Alpha and the Omega—our very beginning and our destination—was proof enough for my parents to overcome the obstacles they encountered.

> "I am the Alpha and the Omega, the Beginning and the End," says the Lord, "who is and who was and who is to come, the Almighty."
>
> REVELATION 1:8 (NKJV)

Moreover, according to the inspired Word of God, "But the fruit of the Spirit is love, joy, peace, longsuffering, kindness, goodness, faithfulness, gentleness, self-control; against such things there is no law" (Galatians 5:22-23, ESV). For without Christ, we are nothing. We cannot live without Him in our life. We exist only because of His will and divine plan. Nevertheless, for me, nothing now seemed to matter. I was happy; I knew no pain, fear, or heartache. I had everything any child could ever want, and for some others, my life was what they dreamed of having. I had a family that showed nothing but love, even through the roughest of times; and even when the storms, clouds, and rain came, nothing seemed to impair the love of my family. My parents appeared to be happier despite what seemed to many as an impossible situation to get through; and me being just a young child, I was nonchalant about what could possibly happen.

It was close to my graduation from elementary school when my mother became terminally ill. I felt the hurt, but I really did not understand what was going on. I only knew that my dad and other family members were sad most of the time. Even though they smiled and laughed constantly, it was obvious that something drastic was happening; and by the frequent whispering, I knew something would happen soon. I knew that my mom and dad loved me and would always be close to me.

I loved going to school, but like many kids in my neighborhood, being home was more fun. I had become the teacher's pet, and I made a lot of friends. I was involved in many of the school's activities. I was a member of the student safety patrol, I joined the music club, and I played the flute and bells. I was also active with the Girl Scouts, and several other school clubs. Although I never really mastered playing the flute, I just wanted to please my parents who were so proud of everything I did in school. After several attempts to play the flute, one day in class the teacher had everyone play their instruments one after the other. I had gotten away with doing just the basics and seriously did not make an effort to master what I needed to do. My teacher knew I was faking it most of the time, just like God knows what we are doing all of the time. God knows when we are true and faithful in our daily living. I did not care about being popular or if I was the best at playing my instrument in class. For me, it was all about my parents and making them proud of what I was able to accomplish, no matter how small. God knows when we are in harmony or when we are just simulating our way through. I believe that we are designed with emotions that help us in determining how and what we do. In our consciousness and God-given capability to determine right from wrong, God has given us favor and blessings to keep us from falling. As my teacher approached me, I felt panic; and oh, let me tell you, my heart began pounding faster and faster. Consequently, the sudden feeling of my heart pounding so hard and the sweaty eyebrows resulted in me acting as if I had been playing all the time. I was relieved when the teacher simply said, "Are you okay, Paddy?"

> And this is love: that we walk in obedience to his commands. As you have heard from the beginning, his command is that you walk in love.
>
> 2 JOHN 1:6 (NIV)

> Children, it is your Christian duty to obey your parents, for this is the right thing to do. "Respect your father and mother" is the first commandment that has a promise added: "so that all may go well with you, and you may live a long time in the land."
>
> EPHESIANS 6:1-3 (GNT)

I continued to struggle but learned the importance of paying attention to and following the instructions of my teacher. When concert time came, I knew I had to be a part of the concert. My parents anxiously awaited and told the whole family, including my church family and neighbors, that I was going to be a part of the concert. To my amazement, even my church family was encouraging me to do my best, as they told me how proud they were of me. Watching with the excitement that Christmas time induces, my parents and godparents (my aunt and uncle) smiled with joy as they entered the large crowded assembly room where Pooh (as I was affectionately known) was performing; and that was all that mattered to them. The day of the concert was a fun time. All the students were dressed in uniforms: navy blue skirts and white tops for the girls and navy blue pants for the boys. The assembly room was full of smiling school staff, excited parents, and other students. Little did I know that as the bells rang, the drumbeat grew louder, and the trumpet players played their instruments, I would never feel this excitement again. The excitement was like none I had ever experienced at that point in my life. I was delighted in the fact that I learned to play the flute and also that I was a part of the musical performance that day.

As graduation grew near and my performance with the orchestra was over, my mom's condition had deteriorated to a greater degree. Unfortunately, the doctors did not know what was wrong—test after test with no indication of any developments or improvement. My mom was getting weaker and weaker physically, yet she remained strong in her faith and trust in the Lord. My mom did not let her unknown illness hinder her walk with the Lord. She was always smiling; and I think she worried more about me than her illness or being confined in the hospital. I sadly watched my mom become so ill that she could hardly walk, yet she still smiled every day and always reminded me to pray.

The time of my graduation from elementary school had arrived. For me, climbing and running the busy halls everyday was exciting, but nothing was more exciting than graduation day. Teachers greeting parents and saying farewell to the kids made graduation exciting. For my family, it was yet a struggle in the midst of all the excitement. Mom had become gravely ill, and she was diagnosed with an inoperable form of cancer. My dad really tried to keep his pain hidden, especially when my aunt and uncle would call to check on us. As my mother remained in the hospital, we often went to my godparents' house for Sunday dinner. Cancer was an unknown disease at the time of my mother's illness; and to the amazement of the doctors and attending staff—none of whom were prepared for or certain about its treatment—it kept growing and spreading faster and faster.

Somehow, my mom found the strength and managed to climb three flights of stairs to see her little girl graduate. Life does hand us many challenges as we live each day. However, having the will power to fight and stay the course with the Lord will essentially lead to one's survival. Life presents many facets, whereas we have to fight to win and fight to keep our minds focused on the true, risen King.

As I proceeded to march in the room filled with parents and the school's staff, I was extremely proud of myself. I was even happier when I saw the smiling faces of my parents and godparents as they waved to me. Seeing my mom and dad smile was everything. Aunt Pat and Uncle Rich were there laughing and pointing at me as I marched in, echoing encouraging phrases: "That's our girl," "Lord! Look at Ms. Pooh." Unfortunately, my mom passed away shortly after graduation, and her passing was exceedingly hard on the family. I watched my dad become sad and brokenhearted. Yet, he would still sing "Leaning on the Everlasting Arms" faithfully, and we still attended church regularly. Wholeheartedly, dad knew that leaning on the arms of the Lord would be all that he needed. Leaning on the everlasting arms of God gives us the assurance that through it all God will provide. He will lead us through the valley, over the mountains, and through the wind, rain, snow, and storms of life.

> The eternal God is thy refuge, and underneath are the everlasting arms: and he shall thrust out the enemy from before thee; and shall say, Destroy them.
>
> DEUTERONOMY 33:27

Life without my mom was new to me and my dad because I did not know what to do and neither did he. He now had to nurture a growing, little girl alone. My dad lost the woman he loved—his soul mate, wife, and companion. My dad had been a chef in the navy, and just prior to my graduation, my family attended his retirement banquet. I remember all of the people applauding and commending him for his service and dedication. Seven months later, the same people who partook in my dad's wonderful retirement celebration now ministered to him and helped to take care of him in every possible way. The help received was genuine, as friends and family often gathered at our house to bring food, do chores, and run errands.

While asleep in my bed one night after my mom passed away, a loud bang erupted in the house. Instantly, I awakened in a sheet of fear, as I was afraid and alone. I called out to my dad multiple times but got nothing in return except silence. My bedroom was right next to the bathroom, and I saw the light on. However, my fear was so strong that I could not find the nerve to go to the bathroom and see what was going on. I was only thirteen years old at the time. I dashed to the hallway where the phone was and called our neighbor. I was nervous, and I cried deeply. The night light in the hallway was dim, but I could see it shining brighter than ever. As I stood on the nearby stool, I dialed the neighbor's phone number, exclaiming to him that something was wrong and my dad was not answering me. Upon the neighbor's instructions, I managed to disarm the burglar alarm and go down the stairs to wait by the door for his arrival. Our houses were adjacent, and a simple jump across the banister made it easy for him to get to my house in a flash. Although it was only minutes later, I was told not to go upstairs but to instead call my aunt from the phone in the dining area downstairs.

Aunt Pat was pregnant and expecting her first child; and I did not want to upset her, so I asked to speak to Uncle Rich instead. Well, of course, she knew something was wrong; but she still let me speak to my uncle, and I gave him the news that something was wrong with my dad. My aunt, curious about me calling at such an early hour and the faintness of my voice, asked if I was okay. I explained to her that my dad was just sick, and I wanted to talk to my uncle. She assured me that she would be right there; and she was. Imagine seeing my dad as he lay there with his eyes shut, glasses on, and not saying anything to me as EMS prepared to take him to the hospital. Aunt Pat and Uncle Rich arrived just as EMS was taking my dad away. Sadly, he passed away upon arrival at the hospital.

At that point in my childhood, nothing seemed to matter anymore. I felt so lost and truly did not know where or who to turn to. As a child growing up, all I knew was my mom and dad; I only knew mom and dad, and my favorite aunt and uncle were always close by. This was traumatic for my aunt, as she was expecting her first child, but she still came through for me as always. I often visited my aunt and uncle, and sometimes I spent weekends with them. My aunt was my mom's sister, and she helped nurture me during my formative years and early adulthood. Aunt Pat was not the only adult relative that had an impactful presence in my life. Connie—who was kind of distant but still visible enough for me to dote on—supposedly was a fashion model in New York. It was explained to me that she was my older sister. She visited frequently, although at the time I did not understand why she lived so far away.

There was stillness, and most of the time things appeared to be lifeless in my family now. It was strange, nothing like I had ever known before. There was silence; kids at school now stared at me like I had a disease. People in the store would just stare at me and whisper, while some would even shake their heads. Some people would walk right by me, staring and looking at me. My mom and dad were well known throughout the community and township that we resided in. My family was also well known throughout the church family and also in several of the neighboring communities. I imagine that is why people could be heard softly saying, "Poor kid, poor child, I'm so sorry." While on the way to my dad's funeral, the car was at a standstill due to the traffic light, and a lady came over to the car and conveyed to me her love and condolences. No one knew the lady, but she made it a point to approach the car to speak with me, reaching to hold my hands. Amazingly, she did not hesitate to approach the car I was in given the crowds of people standing on the corner. There were throngs of people standing on the streets as the procession of the funeral cars passed by. It was almost like they were watching for a parade to pass by.

An early lesson that I learned was that angels do exist, and God has His own way of sending people into our lives to help us get through the toughest times and rough points. Amazingly, the window was rolled down and this one lady was holding grocery bags tightly in her arms as she bent over to approach the limousine. For sure, one thing I learned was that treating people right in addition to walking and living according to the Word of God is the right thing to do.

> Let no corrupting talk come out of your mouths, but only such as is good for building up, as fits the occasion, that it may give grace to those who hear. And do not grieve the Holy Spirit of God, by whom you were sealed for the day of redemption. Let all bitterness and wrath and anger and clamor and slander be put away from you, along with all malice. Be kind to one another, tenderhearted, forgiving one another, as God in Christ forgave you.
>
> EPHESIANS 4:29-32 (ESV)

Resulting from the trauma, heartaches, devastation, and painful past, the passing of my parents spurred a new chapter in my life. I now began to think that happiness would never happen again for me. This true story of drama would turn my life upside down and into many shattered pieces, broken hopes, and dreams. To say that my life would become a piece of shattered glass would not truly describe the pain which was to come. As the wind blows from north to south and from east to west, so was my life as it was blown from side to side. Life would soon become shaped and molded into the likeness of what I could only describe at that time as a never-ending whirlwind.

The stronger the wind blew, the harder were the tests, pain, and misery. The story does not end here; it was just beginning. As time passed, I was tossed around from family member to family member, rejected by many, and I even felt as though I was hated. My aunt Pat was suffering from a great deal of stress with her first child on the way; not to mention, the loss of her sister Nora (my mother) and her brother-in-law Jeremiah (often called Uncle Jerry or Unc) just months apart only made things worse. Here she was through it all, trying to take care of me as she always had helped my mother do.

At this point in my life, the rain seemed to keep pouring relentlessly along with never-ending storm winds, thunder, and lightning. The rain was pouring; the rain and thunderstorms were constant, and hail just kept beating on every part of my frame. It was at this stage in my life that I could truly say my life journey began, and it would be a story that would have life-lasting effects on me, my children, grandchildren, friends, and family.

Love was truly my family's heart's desire. My parents shared their love with everyone they knew. The holidays we celebrated together would become our most memorable family times. There were cookouts—chicken, ribs on the grill, fish frying—and dinners at Thanksgiving and Christmas. The kitchen and dining room were always full of food that my parents prepared and set up on the counters. Most of the gatherings were at my parents' house; even church socials were held at our home. I remember ladies from the church always commenting on my mother's specialty: hot buttery rolls. My dad's specialty happened to be mincemeat pies. My dad was the door greeter, and he always greeted everyone with a smile. He offered conversations to anyone, and everyone congregated in the dining room nearby. My mom and dad made celebrations seem so special. I, most of the time, received everything on my wish list for Christmas. If it was not on my list, it was still something I loved having. I had every doll that came out then; if you could name the doll, I guarantee I had it and with multiple matching outfits too. The holidays always had our house filled with the smell of food being cooked in the kitchen; as dad was baking mincemeat pies, mom would be baking the turkey and dressing; and on some occasions, there would be chitterlings boiling on the stove. That was the only part of the cooking and eating that I never did— chitterlings. I never had them on my plate. Apple pie was my favorite.

My role in the kitchen was to just watch everyone cook. Sometimes I got to wash the vegetables or lick the batter from the large, brown mixing bowl after the cake had been mixed and poured into a baking pan. Anytime the doorbell rang, I excitedly ran from the kitchen to see who the next guest would be. Family time was important, as were Sunday morning family devotionals and breakfast prior to leaving for church. Sundays were always a special time—time for family gatherings and occasionally attending the Sunday evening church services. If there was no evening church service we would just go home and have dinner. Interestingly, Sunday was a day of devotion. There was no television on Sundays, just Bible time, homework, and nap time.

My dad would often take me to the nearby convenience store and order me a vanilla float (one scoop of vanilla ice cream and a cup filled with orange soda). Normally, my parents did not allow me to have a lot of sweets, but little did they know that while walking back and forth to school, all the neighborhood kids stopped at the local bakery just blocks away from home for sugar or chocolate chip cookies. Oh yes, we even visited the local convenience store on our way back to school from lunch or on our way home after school, and there was candy for everyone. If you did not have any money, those that did would freely share what they had. Timing was everything because we all knew our parents would be watching the clocks. There was no such thing as payback; we just did what seemed right as we ran home from school laughing and yelling, "See you later!" at each other. This went on for a long time until we all either relocated to another neighborhood or attended another school.

Growing up in my family meant love, kisses, and sharing; it was all I ever knew. The love had no boundaries. My parents reached out to other neighbor families that were less fortunate, often buying food for those who had fallen on tough times. On many occasions, my parents would even take several of the neighborhood kids with us to church. Love meant everything, always given not just to me or my family members but shared with all we met. Reaching out to others and expressing our love with a hug was a way of life for my family.

As the days of my youth morphed into adolescence, adolescence into young adulthood, and young adulthood into full adulthood, the joy I knew and felt slowly faded away just as the day turns into night. The days, months, and years that lay await would suddenly turn into hurt, fear, and pain that would never seem to disappear. My past and the things I knew would soon be washed away like sand that is carried from the seashore into the ocean by undulating waves. Unbeknownst to me was the love of God that would wipe away the tears, hurt, pain, shame, and abuse that was to come. I would find some new relationships that would see me through all the many challenges that life would present. *Will Power: The Call to Rise Above* was being birthed. I would become a new person, I would become stronger, and I would become equipped to stand in the midst of the trials and tests. Significantly, I would find and have a relationship with someone I had always heard of in church or from my parents' teachings. Little did I know that this "someone" loved me so much. He would make the difference in my life, and He gave His life to save many.

Yes, I heard the stories, I read about Jesus in Sunday school, and heard the pastor preach Sunday after Sunday of the love of God; but I did not know the power and grace of God that would guide me in equipping myself with tools for survival. Coping with the loss of both parents was difficult, and my emotions were all over the place. I would feel pain today, sadness tomorrow, and just down right miserable the next day. I was young and did not know how to tell anyone how I was feeling. I thought that if I would explain my feelings no one would care. My aunt Pat always found a way to perk me up, but it was not the same anymore. I felt excruciating pain. There was a void within me, and I noticeably began to feel shameful, especially after the very home I grew up in was lost to foreclosure. I lost my home, my dolls, and everything that ever meant anything to me. I arrived one day from school and the doors were padlocked. I remember there was a bar on the front door, and entry was impossible. Larchwood Avenue seemed different. The neighbors all stood in amazement as I cried, not knowing what to do. My aunt Pat lived nearby; and she arrived soon, as I stood in amazement and cried uncontrollably. I was crying so much that I am sure I was in panic mode.

People in the neighborhood just stared in bewilderment, and I cried even more because I did not know what was happening or why. And with everyone peeking out of their windows or looking on as they drove by, I wondered where I was to go or who I could turn to. Nonetheless, God was still in the midst of my storm. God was taking me to a place that only He could take me. I had to endure the bad weather; I had to let the rain fall, the wind blow, and the hail hit. I had to let it pound against the walls of my heart, and no friend or family member could ever heal the hurt I felt.

I ran to my aunt again, and there I found that going back to the home I knew was never going to happen. My life was taking a turn from love to hate. I became bitter and was so hurt that I started to do things out of spite. It was almost as though I wanted someone else to feel the hurt I was feeling. I began to roll my eyes and talk back when being disciplined. I let my hurt become my attitude. Thank God for my godparents (Aunt Pat and Uncle Rich), who understood me and loved me unconditionally despite my attitude and behavior.

In efforts of bonding closer together, Aunt Pat often shared with me the details of her wedding day and how I acted on that day. I was only five or six years old at the time. She was dressed in her long, laced, white wedding gown and the doors of the church opened and in she walked. She reminded me of how my adolescent, squeaking voice could be heard yelling, "Aunt Pat's the bride," as she came marching down the aisle amid the sea of smiling onlookers, taking time to smile and wave at me. My godparents showered me with love and continued to hug and kiss me as though I was still their little "Pooh" or "Old Soul" as they called me. Chastisement was in order when I did things wrong; but I knew they loved me even more. I loved them as well, but I was hurt and felt so much pain that I did not understand anything. Nothing anyone said mattered or made any sense. I was facing a storm that no man, woman, parent, or grandparent would ever want their child to endure. This was not the path my parents chose for me; but it happened and happened quickly. Now, my life's journey had new meaning. I was unaware, for the most part, of the closeness I had with my aunt and uncle; and that began to change as well.

New relationships, distance, time, and my total being would give birth to a new me—a totally new person. I was completely reborn in every way: physically, mentally, and spiritually. Adjustment and acceptance were added to my new life. I had to adjust to change, the complete change occurring all around me.

As the months passed, my sister Connie became the dominant figure in my life. She relocated back to Philadelphia and became ever present. I was sent to live with Aunt Pat and Uncle Rich for a while, and at this point, I felt something stirring up inside of me. It was a feeling of something strange and abnormal. Family members would gather and talk, yet little could be heard; even if their voices were loud at times, it was not audible to my ears. I sat on the upper staircase from time to time just to hear the conversations. Everyone would talk, after which they either left or stayed to have the usual family dinner, and the previous conversations about me would cease.

Rodney, my cousin and godbrother, had come to live with us after his mother Vivian passed away. Aunt Vivian was my mom's and Aunt Pat's sister. Rodney and I had tons of fun playing on the swing that Uncle Rich built in the basement. We would run back and forth, playing and chasing each other. Unbeknownst at the time was the fact that Rodney was a thespian in the making. Years later, He would be performing in New York on Broadway, starring in several Emmy and Tony Award winning shows. From high school performances to Broadway, Rodney excelled in his dancing and singing. Rodney and I had developed a closeness that would be life-lasting.

I remember when we were assigned to clean the kitchen and take the trash out after dinner. Rodney would always make the task fun. Amazingly, when the time came to take the trash out, Rodney would run around the corner and visit with his friends. On the other hand, I was busy watching the door waiting for his return, and soon thereafter there was Rodney with a pint of vanilla ice cream that he somehow managed to get from the neighborhood store. Dinner was over, and we had dessert; but little did our aunt and uncle know that we were having additional desserts, even pinching off a piece of the cake or pie in the refrigerator.

Now, it was not known to either of us that we would be so close. Only years later would we become closer and inseparable. He would become more of a real brother than anyone else. We never imagined that both our lives would go down similar roads in years to come.

THE JOURNEY BEGINS

I was cast upon You from birth; From my mother's womb You have been my God. Do not be far from me, for trouble is near; And there is no one to help.

PSALM 22:10-11 (AMP)

The time had arrived when I was to relocate away from my hometown, leaving behind my friends, family, and everyone and everything that was close to me. Time was about to write my life's story from beginning to end, with a new cast and production crew included. Time was making the difference as I grew from one stage to the next and from place to place.

The time had arrived when my life's journey would have new meaning in every sense. My journey was going to be like the vows recited in a marital ceremony: for better or worse, richer, or poorer, in sickness and in health until death do us part. Everything I knew before was fading away, and nothing could ever replace the family I knew all my life up to that point. What would be significant as time passed would be the memories of my family, the Sunday morning devotionals, family time, and holiday celebrations. After the loss of my family and home, things really began to turn. Family secrets were unfolding and relationships were changing. When family members returned to their homes after the home-going service of my father, my sister and I seemed to only have my godparents to rely on. I had a large family; but here we stood with weight on our shoulders—mostly the shoulders of my sister—and feelings of loneliness and confusion.

There had been discussions amongst my family members on my relocation and living arrangements. Once again, I was left out of the conversations, despite me and my immediate future being the focal point. Feeling left out was just part of the problem. My aunt Pat throughout the years had become the family's most famous aunt. Everyone loved Aunt Pat and loved visiting with her. Aunt Pat had special food dishes for every child that came to visit. Aunt Pat would always say that nurturing a child was important, and she did this for each child in our family in a special way. When the time arrived for her to give birth to her first child, I remember being so happy because my aunt was very special to me. It is amazing that while she was in college, she would always stop by my house to check on me. She came by daily; not a day went by that she did not visit. I remember one particular night when everyone thought I was upstairs sleeping, but I could not go to sleep because Aunt Pat was supposed to come and tuck me in but had not arrived yet. Aunt Pat did not let me down; she showed up as I sat at the top of the stairs in curious anticipation, sitting and waiting for her to tuck me in. She gently came and tucked me in, giving me a hug and a kiss. This incident would be remembered throughout the years as I grew older, and it was always laughed about whenever the two of us got together. My mom and aunt had a really close relationship, as did my aunt and my dad. I somehow inherited the nickname "Old Soul" from my mom and aunt because of that night. One could hear them laughing time after time in astonishment of how I could always tell when my aunt was nearby. Laughingly, my mom and aunt could be heard from downstairs saying, "That old soul! You can't fool her."

The time arrived when my aunt was days away from giving birth to her first child. How excited I was! All I knew then was that I could help my aunt take care of the new arrival, and that's all that mattered. I remember going to the hospital to see her as she was just about to give birth. I was taken to the hospital to visit Aunt Pat while she awaited the birth of the baby. However, I could not go in the room to see her but could only see her through a window in the hallway. She stood tall, waving and blowing kisses to me. She was dressed in her white, floor-length gown with matching robe and slippers. That seemed to be all that I needed to make me smile right then and also for days to come. I felt better because she was my aunt and I loved her very much. The baby boy, Ricky, was born, and it was a happy yet bittersweet time—a new beginning but also the end. The birth of Ricky occurred after my parents had passed away, and I would never ever experience the real family life that I was accustomed to.

When I got the opportunity to hold the new baby boy, I was so excited. I always called him Baby Red. Ricky always seemed to smile, and I was delighted when the opportunity came in which I could help fix his bottles. I was able to help with whatever I could and whatever small task I was given. Weeks after, it was back to pain after pain; pain I never knew had a welcome mat waiting for me. Not even a toothache or a backache could be compared to what I was about to endure.

The sudden announcement of me and my sister's relocation was horrific. Going away and not knowing if I would see my aunt again brought me to a place where I could not see my way through. Unbeknownst to me, God had His hands stretched out, and He was holding me safe in His arms.

> I lift up my eyes to the hills. From where does my help come? My help comes from the Lord, who made heaven and earth. He will not let your foot be moved; he who keeps you will not slumber. Behold, he who keeps Israel will neither slumber nor sleep. The Lord is your keeper; the Lord is your shade on your right hand. The sun shall not strike you by day, nor the moon by night. The Lord will keep you from all evil; he will keep your life. The Lord will keep your going out and your coming in from this time forth and forevermore.
>
> PSALM 121 (ESV)

It was just days before my sister Connie and I had to prepare to head south to a whole new family, location, and culture that we did not know and had probably seen maybe once or twice on previous summer visits with my mother. Here I am now, all packed up and ready for the train ride to South Carolina. Sad I was, as family members gathered to see me and Connie off to the train station. It was sad, and oh, how I wanted to run away; running far, far away was written in my mind. Although running away was a thought, where I would go was something I now pondered even more. It seemed like everyone that knew my parents in the town at that time, and even my friends, could not help me. I was in distress; I was hurting so deep within. I was only thirteen and there was nothing anyone could do to rid me of that pain.

So there I was, afraid and crying; and now, the person I always knew as my big sister Connie, became my guardian and surrogate mother. I was astonished when my family members, aunts, and uncles all gathered to tell me that Connie was actually my real mother. It had only been six months since the person I knew as my mother had passed away and a few days since the man I had known as my father had passed away. The parents I knew would in my heart be unreplaceable no matter what I was told or given the facts that existed. My aunts and uncles all met and were concerned for my well-being. Nonetheless, the truth had to be told. The secret was told as family members gathered and made decisions for my well-being. The secret was painfully revealed that my big sister was my biological mother. Yet, no one mentioned my biological father or who he was and where he was—just whispers of how I resembled him and had red-brown hair like him. I heard the chattering whispers of how my father had come to visit me during my infancy and earlier childhood life. Now, I had to accept Connie as my real mother and no longer as the distant sister.

Connie was pretty, tall, blessed, and chosen to model in one of the leading New York department stores. Although I hardly saw her, I still admired her because of her beauty and because she brought me gifts whenever she visited. Yet, I had a feeling that something was wrong whenever she visited because her trips were always short, and we never seemed to talk a lot. Mom and dad had very little conversations with her as well. Amazingly, as the time came and the family's secret of me being Connie's daughter was out, it was no longer gossip; it was fact, truth, and reality. The time had arrived and the hands on the clock moved round and round, sometimes appearing to move slowly. The shift in my life and my mother Connie's new life brought about the dark secret of her unquestionably being my biological mother. Wow! What a shocker that was?

As I sat in anger now, I reached a point where I could not cry because my tears had faded away. I was spellbound at the newly discovered facts and disheartened at having to leave Philadelphia, my friends, and the only loved ones I knew. This brought such pain and hurt, the type that time never seemed to heal. But through it all, still being birthed was *Will Power: The Call to Rise Above.*

As the train rolled out of Thirtieth Street station, the tears returned even more this time—more and more. I could only feel coldness upon my face as the tears began to roll. All the seated passengers in the train watched and stared at me and my mother as we boarded the train. I was crying without making a sound; the tears just wouldn't stop, and the more I tried to hold them back the more they began to roll down my small face. The noise of the bellowing train horns meant nothing to me. I did not care about the other people boarding the train, shoving and throwing their bags and suitcases in the overhead bins; I just had to get on the train. There were people standing by the tracks, waiting to greet their friends and family. Just as we had to say good-bye, there were others seated and standing by the windows doing the same. I was so hurt that I could not even face Aunt Pat and Uncle Rich as they stood there smiling and waving at me through the window. The longer I watched them stand there and wave, the more I cried. With steady streams of tears flowing down my cheeks, I watched as they blew me a kiss and finally walked away. My mother seemed a little mesmerized for a while, as we could hear the train conductor shouting for all to come aboard; and all you could hear was the sound of the train's wheels slowly moving from the station.

For a while, we both just looked out of the windows; and as the train reached other stations, we gazed at the people getting on and off the train, tossing their bags everywhere. As night fell, I finally settled in my seat, almost speechless, yet with a gaze in my eyes—carefully studying each station as people boarded and alighted, with the conductor calling out each and every stop. Connie sat silently for most of the trip. She did ask me if I was okay and if I wanted something to eat. Yes, I wanted something alright—I wanted my aunt and uncle, my mom and dad, and more of what I knew. Food was nothing at that point. We went to the dining car, but the food was not the same. The soda was just soda, and it seemed so flat. After a few sips I was done. Then we moved through the cars and back to our seats for the journey ahead.

Sadly, the memory of Aunt Pat waving goodbye remained etched in my head. I remember my aunt waving goodbye through the living room window. Whenever I used to visit her, she would look through the window as I got in the car to return home. I am sure tears were in her eyes as they were in mine; and as she smiled, she softly advised me to always call her and that she would love me no matter where I was. She gave me assurance for my new life ahead, telling me that she would always be with me. I had no fight in me. I felt emptied, all alone, and sad. Yet, God was there all the time, just sitting high and stretching His hands, His love, and protection around me. I did not know or understand how God worked, but I'm grateful He had me in His hands. For what lay ahead, only God could and would bring me to a place called T.H.R.O.U.G.H. I just had to make it through in order to get there.

Leaving Philadelphia was difficult for both Aunt Pat and me. I was her little Ms. Pooh, and she was my favorite aunt. At this point, there was much uncertainty toward my future. Moreover, God who had a plan for my life was still at work; but I just didn't know it. I did not understand or realize how our mighty God was the Alpha and Omega, my beginning and my end. As time moved on, the pain became harder and more difficult to handle. I became rebellious, and I hated my new family and friends. I hated everything: the food, water, sodas, and clothes. I mean everything! I truly hated everything. The environment was a complete 180, and I hated it just for that. Plain and simple, I just hated it period— everyone and everything there.

Although I had come to this place on several prior occasions, this did not in any way feel like home. There were no street lights or neighborhood kids to run and play with; and most importantly, my dolls were missing.

In addition to that, I could not have birthday parties with all the kids from the neighborhood anymore. I was lost, and all I knew was that this was going to be my home from now on; and I hated it. I hated it! The love, peace, and happiness I once knew, now became anger and bitterness; this had become a play in my life, and my role would be that of the main star. After just four months after my arrival to South Carolina, I began to have many thoughts of running away. Finding an empty train car and just riding away in it had become my daily plan. How and where I would go became so frightening, as were the thoughts of being all alone. At this age and point in my life, I felt that my journey would continue to be a struggle of survival. I had little, if any, will power; everything just felt void.

Although I attended church regularly, I sat on the front row and heard every ministered sermon, yet that did not seem to matter. I still felt lost; I was in pain and did not understand how I could end up in what felt like such a desolate state. I was confused because my new family was not adding up to all that I was told it would be. There were no family gatherings as in the past or decorating the Christmas tree with the multi-colored lights, ornaments, and angel hair around the branches; it was now just a tree with mere decorations on it. Even the few lights did not seem bright. In fact, it was to me a tree without significance standing in the middle of the window. If there were presents under the tree, there was no excitement; and everyone just gazed at the gifts, sitting there, wondering what they were. This did not excite me, as I felt nothing inside of me.

There were no more family get-togethers where my mother, aunt, and I would gather in the kitchen to cook our favorite foods. The scent of my dad's mincemeat pie was gone; mom's homemade rolls and the turkey in the oven were all a thing of the past. No more Oreo cookies and milk with my cousin, or trying to ride his oversized bike. When I was at the stage of where I thought I finally was able to ride his bike, one day I turned a corner with it and ran smack dab into a small-framed lady holding bags in her hands. Imagine that and how shocked I was as I heard my cousin laughing and running down the street to meet me. All of that was gone now—the memories, nostalgia, and everything else.

It was now more of a chore to help in the kitchen, compared to the fun it was in the past when I felt like I belonged there with my family. I always had a place in the kitchen with my mom and aunt as the various events and meals were being prepared. I was taught at a young age how to wash the dishes, and my parents would stay close and make fun of me as I played with the suds. It was all gone, and now all I had were memories of days gone by. Connie was often on the move, therefore leaving me with people I did not like. The reality was that I really did not want to like them. I had so much bitterness and hatred for everyone, that I did not think anything could bring back the happiness that I once enjoyed in my old life. It just did not matter to me what anyone said; if it did not spell "back to Philadelphia," believe me, it meant nothing, nothing at all.

The inner part of my total being felt so void; it was hurting relentlessly. The pain grew deeper and deeper, and there was no hope in sight. Despite this fact, there was something in the middle of my stomach that just did not allow me to give up in living this way. I felt the need and desire amid all this to struggle to find contentment. Thank God for the will power and call to rise above what I was suffering through. I had no idea that someone greater than all the problems, hurt, and discontentment was on my side. Such as life would have it, I just had to find a way to live and accept the conditions.

No one seemed to care about how hurt I was, as the adults just kept moving along with their normal routines; they gave me chores to do, sent me to school, and made me attend the local church on Sundays. Little did I know that there was a shadow, hope, and someone that was bigger than anyone else, who cared about me. He unconditionally loved me and was watching me all along. I had to find a place in my heart to let Him in, and let Him dry my tears. His name is Jesus, and I would learn more of His love and amazing grace as time moved on.

As the months and years spent in my new location passed by, I finally made a few friends, even though it seemed like no matter what I did someone was always watching me. I could not find peace with being watched all the time. I was accustomed to laughter and neighborhood kids running up and down the streets. For my fifth birthday, every child in my neighborhood came to my birthday party; the dining room was full, wall to wall with gifts and children. My mom and aunt would have lemonade and cookies prepared on our patio for me and my friends on weekdays after school. Funny thing, one day I told everyone I was having a tea party at my house, but I forgot to ask my parents. The kids started showing up, and my mom and aunt laughed and said, "Old Soul, you having a tea party?" And yes, I did. I had a tea party full of love and fun.

Now, I had reached a point where I did not know how I would survive. God's love was with me. God sees our heart, and He feels the tears that drop from our eyes. God is all we need and will forever be Lord of lords,

King of kings. He is the one and only one that our hope can be formed on. Learning all this would come years later in my life.

I truly struggled to survive. Later on, as the years passed, friends were coming around, and I could at least go to the local store which was in walking distance. I started to go to more local stores. I went on regular shopping trips and attended church occasionally. Even though it felt as if I was still missing something, my pain was slowly starting to fade. I was seeing light, I had become eager, and life was having new meaning and purpose. I began to feel a level of will power and knew that I was being given the opportunity to rise above all that I had endured up until that point. Amazingly, the storm—that had previously arisen and which I thought was moving away—was not over. The storm was going to take a new turn; the winds were going to blow harder and louder. This was a time in my life when I was going to hurt until once again I would not be able to cry anymore.

There would be times when I would feel like I had no more water in me to make the tears stream down my face. There would be so much pain in the days ahead that only God's love and power would help bring me through. I would learn what "will power" really meant.

Although things had turned around, another turn was coming swiftly, and it would hit me hard and in a hurry. It was a tornado; it felt like a torrential hurricane or even a tsunami. Wild fire would begin to burn away inside of me, and who I was would struggle to live. Life was going to teach me how to adapt and equip myself for the battle of a lifetime that was rapidly approaching. Little did I know that I could and would win the battle for survival, unconditional love, and happiness. The battle was not really mine; it was and had already been won on Calvary! God was my hope, my true guide, and sunshine. It was through the death of Jesus, His burial, and resurrection that I would receive the strength to survive. The victory to rise above it all was because of His love and who He had destined me to become.

As the days turned into months, I reconnected with my aunt Pat via frequent phone conversations. We talked more frequently, always laughing and telling each other how much we missed each other. I enjoyed talking to her often, and that meant and made all the difference. I reached a place of comfort where I began to attend and enjoy going to church on Sundays. I think that sometimes it was because I enjoyed how the ladies would call me "you child" and beckon me to come to their stands and fill my plate with delicious food, homemade cakes, pies, fried chicken, ham, and a host of other home cooked delicacies that were served after the church services. The aroma of the food would fill the church during service, and you could see people constantly going in and out of the sanctuary to make preparation for the subsequent meal after service. Sharing meant a lot, and the people were so generous that it reminded me of the family times that I had in my early childhood.

I later joined the choir, and this brought a sense of belonging; somehow, it felt like I had filled a void. I was extremely engaged in the services and programs; and I began to enjoy attending church regularly again. I was finding peace and comfort, and I had friends now. I began to meet people who seemed concerned and even cared about who I was and what I was going through. The invitation to be a part of the church family was a reminder of the church family in Philadelphia that I felt so far and distant from. As time passed, I later went on serving on many of the church auxiliaries.

On the other hand, attending school was not so exciting. I did what I had to do and just wanted it to be over as well. Despite making new friends, school was not the most pleasant setting. The teachers were always yelling, and kids would also run around yelling and talking very loudly. Standing in the doorway of the classroom, the teachers would just stare at us and occasionally command one of the children to stand up or to leave the room. Attending school during the time when segregation in the South was prevalent was a tremendous shock. I had never attended a school in which one race was such a dominant majority, and this was surely a new experience. I began to dislike going to school because either many of the African-American children were targeted in the classrooms, or we would find ourselves being suspended for what seemed to be no reason.

I had my proverbial traveling shoes on and was always looking forward to returning to my hometown and family one day. I had never imagined that life could be as complicated as it was after I was forced to move south. On the other hand, life would become unfathomably rewarding. Neither could I imagine that life after relocating to South Carolina would one day be worth all the pain and hurt that I had endured. It was never imaginable that God would choose me for Kingdom building.

Growing up in the church during my time spent in Philadelphia meant a lot to me; it was hope, and it brought joy to my family to see me involved in the many activities that I enjoyed. Being unprepared for the new direction that my life had taken and always having my traveling shoes on did not make my new life or new home any better, shorter, or more painless. I had to buckle up my shoes and learn to develop into a person that would stand the tests and the trials. In reality, I had to learn—much like a mother travailing in childbirth—that through all the physical and mental pain, you have to have faith and trust in order to enjoy a victorious outcome.

Reaching a point and time in my life where all I wanted was to be free and at peace with myself and the things of my past, I wanted the past to just be the past and go away. Nothing was more important than living in the newness I had found. I no longer wanted the pain of the past constantly piercing my heart. I could not stand being a prisoner anymore, always feeling trapped inside. I was determined to escape the turmoil that previously held me in a place of darkness. I was ready to fight and make the heartaches disappear. Reaching a point of weakness emotionally and physically, I had to make a decision, fight back the pain, or let the pain continue to distract me. I made the choice to fight, and I could fight now because I was so sick and worn out from the hurt and the misery of my past. Suddenly, I had given birth, the hardest contraction was taking place inside of me, and buried deep within me was *Will Power: The Call to Rise Above*. I had to come to grips with myself, and I truly had a calling to rise above any circumstance or situation that presented itself in my life.

A person's life is like grass. Like a flower in the field it flourishes, but when the hot wind blows by, it disappears, and one can no longer even spot the place where it once grew. But the Lord continually shows loyal love to his faithful followers, and is faithful to their descendants, to those who keep his covenant, who are careful to obey his commands. The Lord has established his throne in heaven; his kingdom extends over everything.

PSALM 103:15-19 (NET)

I had already won; but because of what the adversary had in my view, all I could see was defeat. Yet, all the while, *Will Power: The Call to Rise Above* was instilled deep down inside of me. Did the adversary like the fact that I now saw the light or that I could and would fight with all the strength that God gave me to rise above? God was busy preparing, training, and showing me how to become victorious. Was the battle over? Not by any stretch of the imagination, and it actually got harder; but my determination was stronger. It was like the fresh air we breathe every day, and the sound of the birds chirping every morning outside my window. It was the joy of the Lord. Celebrate Jesus with me; for He is awesome, and He is marvelous. It doesn't matter how hard the rain falls, just know that Jesus paid the price. He was hung high, stretched wide, mocked, and tormented for you and me. When in doubt, know that you can do whatever you set your mind to. I had to learn through all the trials and circumstances how to listen for the voice of the Lord rather than continuously listening to Satan with his riddles. As I continued to mature, I was able to discern the Spirit of the Lord as he spoke.

> Do not conform to the pattern of this world, but be transformed by the renewing of your mind. Then you will be able to test and approve what God's will is—his good, pleasing and perfect will.
>
> ROMANS 12:2 (NIV)

With the assurance and the guidance of the Holy Spirit, we are assured sweet and true victory. We are victorious no matter what we come up against because of the price Jesus paid on the cross. Jesus suffered false accusation for crimes He did not commit, yet he had compassion toward everyone.

> And Jesus, when he came out, saw much people, and was moved with compassion toward them, because they were as sheep not having a shepherd: and he began to teach them many things.
>
> MARK 6:33-35

The suffering of Jesus on the cross was horrific, but because of His suffering and love, all mankind has the promise of eternal life.

> The one who is victorious will, like them, be dressed in white. I will never blot out the name of that person from the book of life, but will acknowledge that name before my Father and his angels. Whoever has ears, let them hear what the Spirit says to the churches.
>
> REVELATION 3:5-6 (NIV)

Jeremiah 29:11 declares, "For I know the thoughts that I think toward you, says the LORD, thoughts of peace and not of evil, to give you a future and a hope" (NKJV). Just as God spoke to the people of Babylon through the prophet Jeremiah and promised them that He would allow them to return back home if they would only endure the seventy years of travailing during the Babylonian Captivity, God reassured me that I would be okay even though troubles would come; and He would have my back and cover me because the blood of Jesus was shed for me. His blood was shed even when I was a sinner and had no clue who He was. The assurance and promises of the Lord God Almighty is all one can ever hope for and ever need to get to the place called T.H.R.O.U.G.H.

I reached a place where everything seriously shifted. There was no doubt that something unique was taking place; and I was virtually clueless as to exactly what it was and what was about to become. Internally, I knew something was changing and happening to me. Strength was now becoming my friend. I could climb the mountains; I had been in the valley for far too long. I struggled to walk through the cold, snow, rain, and wind. I believed, and I acquired hope. Although all I could see at this point were clouds, I felt the winds blowing softly from the south to the north and from west to the east; and the winds kept blowing, shifting my life's journey. The winds were shifting, and my life was turning around, as was my character and all that I had experienced. As the wind blew, so did the sweet whispers of the Lord. God continued to remind me that I had a choice, and that I was free to move and get up from drooping on a road marked for failure. The storm was now over; and I was prepared to move forward. Although the storm was over, my faith would continue to be tested as the adversary continued to lay in wait to distract me as he had done in the past.

> Be sober and alert. Your enemy the devil, like a roaring lion, is on the prowl looking for someone to devour. Resist him, strong in your faith, because you know that your brothers and sisters throughout the world are enduring the same kinds of suffering. And, after you have suffered for a little while, the God of all

grace who called you to his eternal glory in Christ will himself restore, confirm, strengthen, and establish you. To him belongs the power forever. Amen.

1 PETER 5:8-11 (NET)

I knew I was on a better path, and I could now see a brighter day. God always has a plan for His children. It is when our lives don't seem to go the way we wish or think that we must learn and know that God is still holding the master plan. The remote control and blueprint of our destiny are in His hands. He's our solid rock, King of kings, and strong and mighty Lord; we have the power He has given to us. Jesus, the solid rock, paid for our salvation and for the very things we wrestle with. We are free only if we believe and use it.

There is no other; no one paid the price like Christ did for our life. Why not live and enjoy Jesus, His love, and His many blessings? Yield not to what the adversary may say, attempt, or even do. Know and trust God through all things, making it your practice to thank Him even when you go through and can't even see your way. Nothing is greater than God's love and His promise. Trust Him, knowing who He is, and love Him in every possible way. Finding and having a relationship with our heavenly Father is the greatest and best relationship you could and will ever have. Friends come and go, family come and go, but God's love stays, and it stays throughout eternity; His love is everlasting.

Although, I felt abandoned for so long, God never gave up on me or my future. God was preparing my life in a way that would become greater than I could or would ever imagine. Despite feeling trapped, God had a plan—a script already written for me. There was sickness, death, pain, and sorrow after sorrow; but God was preparing me for another place, time, and for greater works.

> It is for freedom that Christ has set us free. Stand firm, then, and do not let yourselves be burdened again by a yoke of slavery.
>
> GALATIANS 5:1 (NIV)

> The Spirit of God, the Master, is on me because God anointed me. He sent me to preach good news to the poor, heal the heartbroken, announce freedom to all captives, and pardon all prisoners. God sent me to announce the year of His grace — a celebration of God's destruction of our enemies — and to comfort all who mourn, to care for the needs of all who mourn in Zion, give them bouquets of roses instead of ashes, messages of joy instead of news of doom, a praising heart instead of a languid spirit. Rename them "Oaks of Righteousness" planted by God to display His glory."
>
> ISAIAH 61:1-7 (MSG)

Glory be to God! His instructions are life-lasting, and it is imperative to apply them daily. This is who I am. I am a child of the King and a princess. My life is in His hands. My friends, magnify the Lord and think now about a situation or circumstance that you may have gone through or may be going through now. Imagine if you will, a time when you were sick or a family member was ill and nothing seemed to work. Reflect now, if you will, on a time when you were hurt, brokenhearted, ashamed, ignored by someone, laughed at, or rejected. Even consider a time when you may have lost a loved one. No matter how gruesome or tortuous your circumstance may have been, none of your experiences could or would ever compare to the feelings that Jesus experienced as He was led to Calvary. Think now how you came through the situation and who brought you through it. Our Lord is Yahweh (the One who is always near), Alpha and Omega (our very beginning and end), Adonai (Lord, ruler, and creator of everything), Yahweh Rohi (the Lord our shepherd), Yahweh Rapha (the Lord our healer), Yahweh Jireh (the Lord our provider), Yahweh Shalom (the Lord our peace), El-Olam (the everlasting God), El-Roi (the strong one who sees), and El-Shaddai (God almighty). Jesus is everything we need, and He gave his life for the sake of the world.

There is no one who could love us as much as our heavenly Father who watches over us day after day and night after night. Oh, how wonderful to know that through it all, Jesus our Savior still lives. Trust Him, love Him, obey Him, and give Him all the praise you have. I have learned that it is such a blessing and honor to celebrate the wonderful Savior. Satan can't bless you, but he will try to make you believe that he can. His goal is only to deceive you and sway your focus away from the Lord. Trust and believe in the King of kings, and He will bring you through. In all of the dilemmas and difficulties that we experience, it is important to know that God is preparing us for the place called T.H.R.O.U.G.H.

Separation:

The Test, Trial, and Travailing

———— - ————

As the years progressed, life began to take on a new meaning; or should I say, I discovered a new meaning to life. I still longed for the love and affection I grew up knowing but within me was birthed a new me, a new lady, and a new person. I did not understand nor had I read about the new birth. I simply knew something had changed both physically and mentally. It was deep within me and no one could change what I was feeling now. I just knew that life was not going to be the same. I felt the shift, the rapid change; and I realized I had options to choose from. Whereas in the past, I always thought that nothing mattered because things had been tough for so long and everything was a true twist of fate.

I could either move with the change or get lost through it and the mess, hurt, pain, sorrow, and all the past drama that had occurred in my life. There was so much drama that at this point in time, I could have produced a top-selling Broadway play. I was ready to step out of the muddy water. I felt newness in my steps and direction. I felt like moving from this station and time, walking with a greater strength and knowledge like I never felt before. Where was I going? With whom and to whom was I talking with to tell my story? Hung on the road signs of my journey, it is now that I begin to feel compelled to share my story, which is my testimony. I can tell of God's love toward me despite the mess I had become, or one would say, allowed the adversary to make me believe I had become.

Even through the negative and "stinking thinking" behavior I had acquired, God still cared for and loved me all the more. I often felt like life was dictating things to me in a way that I would never overcome. Life was telling me, "Pat, you have been thrown a monkey wrench, twists, and turns, which will all lead to Nowhere Boulevard." Yet, lingering in my mind was the question: What are you going to do about it? But a friend showed up—someone who had been with me all this time, and I was just so blindsided that I could not see or feel His presence. Jesus was with me every step, every day—noon and night. When the winds blew so strong, He was waving His hands over my head, and I just needed to look up and stop looking down. Remembering the days when I was really sinking deep into depression because things just did not seem to be going my way, I literally would always look down or away—almost as if I was looking down to the ground or floor for answers and some semblance of hope. I just could not face reality. What was so amazing is the fact that on many occasions I found myself constantly hitting or stumping my toe on the corner of a sharp object, hard enough to bruise my toe more painfully each time.

I noticed that this was happening way too much, and the pain was getting more painful each time. God, at work in me, caused me to stop looking down; and I began to walk upright and look to Him whom is seated high above the clouds—sitting high and looking below the heavens onto the earth. He is God Almighty, and He reigns forever. He knows our faults, sees all that we do, and hears all that we say. It is my belief that God was working on my behalf and wanted me to engage in more communication with Him. I was looking in the wrong direction for help. Our help comes from above—the gift of life from the One who created the heavens and the earth.

So, why was I looking down? Well, that is what the adversary will make you do when your heart hangs heavy and your mind is clouded. He wants you to be about Him and not just about the blessings He can provide. In all the fear, hurt, shame, disappointments, and everything that could go wrong, all I could wonder and think about was the same question over and over: What are you going to do about this situation and these circumstances? Ironically, at the end of that question came another question: How am I going to move forward using the power the Lord God gave me to become victorious? Victorious? Who, me? Not even a thought. Luke 10:19 says "Behold, I give unto you power to tread on serpents and scorpions, and over all the power of the enemy: and nothing shall by any means hurt you." I was so blind and afflicted by hurt, shame, and abuse that I did not know what the word victorious meant. Somehow, oddly enough, lost in my memory was the very childhood prayer I was taught and recited nightly:

Now, I lay me down to sleep,

I pray the Lord my Soul to keep;

If I die before I wake,

I pray the Lord my soul to take.

This prayer had become a rehearsal, which was not a bad thing because at the end it would be my strength. It would give me strength as I uttered the words daily, even in my childhood. God heard my heart even then. He was part of my daily meal and routine, and He was also my weapon of survival to see me through the many days ahead. Through God's grace and His unwavering compassion, He empowers His children with knowledge, tools, and provisions. So, why then do you and I doubt, fear, or think that we cannot get through? Satan's "stinking thinking", trickery, mind games, and darts, cloud our thoughts and beings. I had all the wrong thoughts, so I could not come up with anything at the time except a wrong answer to who I was and who I would become in the years to come. Romans 12:2 tells us, "And be not conformed to this world: but be ye transformed by the renewing of your mind, that ye may prove what is that good, and acceptable, and perfect, will of God." Had I followed this instruction—wow, what a difference I could have made! But just like a baby learning to eat and drink, I had to learn to hear the voice of my Father guiding me and providing for me despite my weak state of being.

I had not developed enough from a mental standpoint to use the power that lay within me from birth, so it remained incipient. Moreover, God has seen me through every struggle and circumstance. God knows who I am.

God has also seen you and many others through tough times as well. On the other hand, what might seem like tough times are merely God's way of getting our attention or just tests of our faithfulness. Despite the hard times we face, everything occurs in God's timing. He controls the clock and our destiny. I am ever so grateful to know the Lord and the fact that He loves me through all my wrongdoings. I truly have a song of praise—a hymnal of praise in my mind, mouth, and daily routine. Aren't you glad that God is able to do all things? It is my hope that people all over the world—regardless of their social status, race, gender, and religion—would take a stand, unite, and fight for the gift (the life) given to us by our Creator. We have to live it to the fullest and know that we can do all things through Christ (Phil. 4:13). Whatever seems impossible, you have the will power and the call to rise above. Be on guard, stand firm in the faith, be courageous, and be strong. You have God's promise.

God promises that He will always be near, even when the storm clouds hang low and nothing seems to go the way we think it should. Our God is all we need and is never far away. Prayer and faith work wonders. When we are brokenhearted, when we are sad, and when the storm clouds just do not seem to disappear, we can always look to God. He is the light that shines through the dimmest and darkest situations. All you have to do is trust Him, and God will meet you in the midst of the storm. As for myself—and hopefully for you as well—I shall remain standing on the promises of God forever.

STAND THE RAIN

The spring season was here with flowers and trees starting to bloom everywhere. It was not long that I sat quietly, wondering if the rain would stop and the white clouds that always seemed to be stretching enormously high in the sky would appear. Okay, if you must know, yes, I knew the rain would eventually cease and I would see the clouds again. Simply because of the place, time, and challenging situations, the rain seemed to be falling harder and harder from the sky, pounding more in my mind and in my heart. My heart was bleeding for peace, as it was clouded by so many things. There was no peace, nowhere to hide, and no one on earth to tell my sorrows; I felt there was no one who truly cared enough to write a book about my life.

Sitting in the den of my house one day, all I could see passing by were cars along the highway, moving slowly. The front yard of my house was now flooded as the water settled in the doorway. This had happened many times before, but never like on this particular day. Nevertheless, few drivers were still moving along as though the rain was not falling. I could see the cars' windshield wipers going back and forth, moving like the hands on a ticking clock and creating visibility for the cars' drivers. On this day the rain was so heavy that I could feel the raindrops in my thoughts and heart. All I wanted to do was be in the house alone, sit, and just watch TV. I don't drink coffee, and I drink very little hot tea if I ever venture to drink it. For coffee drinkers, this would have been one of those days to enjoy a good cup while just relaxing, sitting back in the recliner and reading a good book, or better yet, meditating on the Word of God. However, my thought at this point in time was that I should take a nap. Funny, taking a nap sounded like a good thing if only I could have allowed my mind and body to get in relaxed mode; it was not a bad thought. I am not one to allow myself to shut things down early in the day, so taking a quick nap was not an option for me. Note, I said, I *don't* allow myself to do so. The thought of watching a good movie did cross my mind. I just could not find anything that really held my interest on this day. I must admit, for me it was working on projects and applications on my computer that did it. I found myself more relaxed as this brought a real sense of comfort to me. Was this the trick of the enemy again, messing with my mind and distracting me away from what God was trying to reveal?

So, here I was, ignoring what God was trying to do in me! I was at a place where meditation was difficult. I could not see anything, and even the TV meant nothing to me. I could not hear the birds chirping or singing to each other, as I did every morning. I could not hear the sound of the hard rainfall upon the roof, nor could I hear anything other than the very struggle I was now enduring, which was beating harder and harder to erase all positive thoughts from my mind. Truth be told, I hardly ever paid attention to or noticed the conspicuously billowing clouds in the sky. Prior to this I was oblivious to the nuances of the weather and only noticed or talked about the weather when others brought it up in conversation. The rain kept falling, and it simply did not matter to me; I felt like a blank slate. So, why was I there, repeatedly having these thoughts, feelings, and insecurities?

> You gave abundant showers, O God; you refreshed your weary inheritance.
>
> PSALM 68:9 (NIV)

I pondered how it was even possible for someone to not notice the rain when it falls. The rain is refreshing and delightful, and it gives birth to nature. The rain is water that produces and replenishes. When we consider the flood during Noah's time, the many hurricanes, and the tornados occurring in various states today, it is not atypical to be reminded that God is Alpha and Omega.

Stroll now with me through the story of Noah, the ark, and the Flood. Noah was chosen by God to perform a special task. He was laughed at, he was the talk of the town, and even his family questioned his actions. I can relate to this story because like Noah, my family and close friends would laugh at me when I went through struggles and hard times and when I decided to live my life differently. Amidst the laughter, I was called crazy, adopted, insane, foolish, and whatever other name they could think of. Was Noah mocked, rejected, and talked about? Did his family and friends laugh? They surely did, yet Noah continued in his quest to obey the Lord in constructing the ark. He let nothing deter him from faithfully following the instructions of God. Noah's friends and family saw only what they wanted to see at the time. However, Noah simply had a strong desire to follow God, and he was determined to be obedient. Are you hearing or following God's instructions? Are you listening to the voice of the Lord as your friends, family, and co-workers talk about and laugh at you behind your back? For most of us, this is not easy. Far too often, we hear the voice of our heavenly Father, but we do not yield to His words out of fear of what others will think or say. What has become important to me now that many years have passed is my knowing and recognizing the voice of my heavenly Father, being a good listener in my mind, and having an open heart.

After losing both of my parents at the age of thirteen, for a long time I struggled to fit in with the in-crowd. I wanted to be one of the popular ones. I wanted to be the best friend. I even struggled to exist within my new family, but little did I know that my heavenly Father was my family. The separation and the distance of my biological family had become harder and harder to deal with. I can imagine how Noah felt leaving behind friends and people he was close to. Yet, Noah believed in God's love. Noah's faith and trust in God led him into believing he would prevail. No matter how hard the storm became or the winds blew, Noah, stretching out on faith through the roughest times, stood on the promises of God.

Even when the clouds grew dark and all he could see was rain and darkness, Noah embraced the storm, winds, and waves that tossed the ark from side to side. Noah stood determined, steadfast, and unmovable on the promise and instructions of the Lord. Can you stand as Noah, believing and not doubting the Word of the Lord? Can you stand tall through the heartache and pain? Can you stand being laughed at, lied on, talked about, and having your so-called friends turning their backs on you?

Can you stand as a true solider, arming yourself with the Word of God and being anchored in the Lord? The answer is *yes* because we have the gift that sets us free, which is the gift of salvation. Salvation offers hope, joy, and happiness and frees us from anything that will prevent us from having eternal life with the Lord. Stand on the promises of God, and He will not forsake you nor leave you if you believe in Him. Do you believe? I do! Noah was a righteous man; blameless, he walked faithfully with God.

> And it came to pass, when men began to multiply on the face of the earth, and daughters were born unto them, That the sons of God saw the daughters of men that they were fair; and they took them wives of all which they chose. And the Lord said, My spirit shall not always strive with man, for that he also is flesh: yet his days shall be an hundred and twenty years. There were giants in the earth in those days; and also after that, when the sons of God came in unto the daughters of men, and they bare children to them, the same became mighty men which were of old, men of renown. And God saw that the wickedness of man was great in the earth, and that every imagination of the thoughts of his heart was only evil continually. And it repented the Lord that he had made man on the earth, and it grieved him at his heart. And the Lord said, I will destroy man whom I have created from the face of

the earth; both man, and beast, and the creeping thing, and the fowls of the air; for it repenteth me that I have made them. But Noah found grace in the eyes of the Lord. These are the generations of Noah: Noah was a just man and perfect in his generations, and Noah walked with God. And Noah begat three sons, Shem, Ham, and Japheth. The earth also was corrupt before God, and the earth was filled with violence. And God looked upon the earth, and, behold, it was corrupt; for all flesh had corrupted his way upon the earth. And God said unto Noah, The end of all flesh is come before me; for the earth is filled with violence through them; and, behold, I will destroy them with the earth. Make thee an ark of gopher wood; rooms shalt thou make in the ark, and shalt pitch it within and without with pitch. And this is the fashion which thou shalt make it of: The length of the ark shall be three hundred cubits, the breadth of it fifty cubits, and the height of it thirty cubits. A window shalt thou make to the ark, and in a cubit shalt thou finish it above; and the door of the ark shalt thou set in the side thereof; with lower, second, and third stories shalt thou make it. And, behold, I, even I, do bring a flood of waters upon the earth, to destroy all flesh, wherein is the breath of life, from under heaven; and everything that is in the earth shall die. But with thee will I establish my covenant; and thou shalt come into the ark, thou, and thy sons, and thy wife, and thy sons' wives with thee. And of every living thing of all flesh, two of every sort shalt thou bring into the ark, to keep them alive with thee; they shall be male and female. Of fowls after their kind, and of cattle after their kind, of every creeping thing of the earth after his kind, two of every sort shall come unto thee, to keep them alive. And take thou unto thee of all food that is eaten, and thou shalt gather it to thee; and it shall be for food for thee, and for them. Thus did Noah; according to all that God commanded him, so did he.

GENESIS 6

There was not much chit-chat taking place, but Noah, being anchored, talked with the Lord instead of chatting with those who mocked him. He grew stronger in his faith and trust in the Lord, working hard as commanded and not paying heed to the mockery and raillery from the onlookers. We have to teach ourselves to be in tune with God when He speaks to our hearts, believing with all our being as Noah and many others in history have done. Hope, joy, and peace—it is all ours if we ask and open our hearts to receive the blessings and gifts that our Lord patiently waits to bestow on His children.

And my God will meet all your needs according to the riches of His glory in Christ Jesus.

PHILIPPIANS 4:19 (NIV)

I'm reminded of the song "Encourage Yourself" written by Donald Lawrence. Although, many of my friends and family members turned away from me, some have now turned to me for advice or even my attention. But I have now found the saving grace and love from God that allows me to be healed from the previous pain and not hold on to the bitterness of the past. No, this did not stop people from laughing as I walked past them, but I have the strength to get out of the place called "despair." Encouraged I have become, and also I have found what was lost. Because of the love of our heavenly Father, I have enough reinforcement, wisdom, love, and willingness to help those who have turned against me.

> Praise be to the God and Father of our Lord Jesus Christ! In his great mercy he has given us new birth into a living hope through the resurrection of Jesus Christ from the dead, and into an inheritance that can never perish, spoil, or fade. This inheritance is kept in heaven for you, who through faith are shielded by God's power until the coming of the salvation that is ready to be revealed in the last time.
>
> 1 PETER 1:3-5 (NIV)

Something had changed, and something was turning inside of me like a windmill. Although silent, something was giving new meaning to the pain and heartache I'd felt for such a long time. Something within was fighting, and it awakened the giant sleeping within me. Like many people often do, I had ignored the beauty and significance of the rain. Think now with me of how the adversary will block your vision and your focus on the glory and wonders of the Lord. Yes, it does happen when we allow the adversary to enter our very thoughts and penetrate our minds with his fiery darts and negative thinking. The adversary wants to control our minds, what we say, and what we do. I can remember hearing several times in various conversations where people declared, "Don't let him ride. He'll want to drive." The key is to be able to discern what is coming from God our Father and what is coming from the adversary. Knowing makes all the difference as I can attest to having witnessed the adversary's work over and over. The voice of deception in your ears can paint some really ugly pictures in your mind. What's funny is that the pictures that the adversary paints will have you thinking, *Oh this is awesome!* He will leave you hanging all alone, wondering which way to turn. He will burden you with loads of heartache if you let him. It is important to use the power—will power, that is, and answer the call of God to rise above. It is your gift from God!

One thing is for sure, the closer I became to knowing that I was being set apart as one of God's chosen servants, the more I focused on the wonders of God. No way did the attacks stop coming. My thoughts got cloudier sometimes, and interestingly, while writing this book I was under attack. I am commissioned now, and I must endure the many constant hardships, trials, tests, pain, and despair. I know the meaning of standing on the solid rock. I know how to stand and be still. I am determined to live so that my life is pleasing to God and I can be an example of a model Christian and the wonders of the Lord God.

> Ye are of God, little children, and have overcome them: because greater is he that is in you, than he that is in the world.
>
> 1 JOHN 4:4

Noah stood when the ark landed and looked over the land. As a servant of the Lord God, I can say today that I am standing, looking to God, and thanking Him for bringing me through the many storms thus far. I am even thanking Him for providing me with the strength, hope, and determination for Kingdom building. Amazing grace is truly my friend, and Noah clearly had amazing favor and grace, one that followed him for the rest of his life. Through it all, Noah was called to rise above it all: wind, rain, storm, laughter, and mockery. He never doubted but looked up to God instead.

Just as God gave His assurance and hope to Noah, He has given it to me too. I went through a time when I was abused both physically and mentally. Again, who could I tell my story to? I thought, *Would anyone believe that I was being molested or abused?* I kept the few incidents to myself, and as a result this began a new way of life. It was all I knew, and I had no one to tell the story to so I accepted it and moved on to the next phase in my life. I felt locked in a place that seemed hopeless; and no one was there but me. It was a place of great struggle just to live or be free. Inside my heart, a small part of me cried silently into the stillness and darkness of many nights. During the stillness of the night when I cried silently through it all, the healing rain did fall. God's grace and mercy were the only assurances I needed as the storm passed over and I kept journeying to a place called T.H.R.O.U.G.H.

Connie, my biological mother, who I began to know as my mother just a couple of years prior, suddenly passed away. Although it was years later, Connie and I would enjoy time with each other as she frequently visited me and my sons, especially during the Christmas and Thanksgiving holidays. After years of living in the South, Connie had relocated back to our hometown of Philadelphia, where she even got married. The excitement of seeing her get off the train when she came to visit was exhilarating, as she always looked so refined. We had good visits, but some consisted of the typical mother and daughter relationship in which parents and children don't always see eye to eye.

Connie was one of the first females in the Church of God in Christ denomination to be ordained as a minister of the gospel. I remember her trial sermon, "The Prodigal Child Returns." I had never seen or heard her minister with such force before, and what an exciting time it was! Her only biological brother arrived from Hawaii, and we both sat among the congregation in amazement at how God had chosen and worked through her.

Connie was a true warrior for Christ. On one Sunday afternoon after just having come home from the hospital some days back, she had to return to the hospital as her health was failing and she was getting weaker by the minute. Upon examination of my mother, the doctor asked her how old she was, and her reply astonished him so much that he was speechless. She was sixty-eight years old, but she looked as though she was still a New York model. She looked at the doctor and asked him right then if she was dying, and he announced that she was dying— from cancer. When the world was closing in on her, lying prostrate on the floor before the Lord became more of her daily diet.

Here I was now with the loss of another mother (this time my biological mother), yet there was so much gained from getting to know her. Her guidance, Bible teachings, and prayers meant everything to me; and they were the tools I needed to be in fellowship with the Lord. I began to really miss Connie. It was hard for a while as I often heard the sound of the trains pass by; and as I watched the passengers board, I reminisced on the good memories of days gone by—memories that I will forever hold in my heart. Thank God for a prayerful and loving woman—a woman of God that never gave up, even when I was in very unappreciative and most uncooperative behavior.

Connie's passing was harder for me to handle because I had just begun to know her as my friend, my confidant, and most importantly my mother. What was so heartbreaking was the fact that there was nothing I could do to help her recover from the breast cancer that had spread from head to toe throughout her entire body. The hurt was overwhelming, but because of her, thank God, I had reached a point where going to church was a passion for me. I began to read the Bible avidly, and I even started collecting various versions of the Bible.

Five years after the passing of my mother, I was joined in holy matrimony to a wonderful man named

Robert. One night after dinner during our second year of marriage, Robert arose from the table rapidly and hurried to the bedroom. This was very unusual for him; and I followed him, only to find him sitting on the bed just staring out of the window. As I began to query him about his behavior I realized that something was wrong. He was rushed to the hospital, and his blood pressure did not even seem to stabilize when the medics gave him medication during the ambulance ride to the hospital. After arriving at the hospital, it was determined that he would undergo triple bypass surgery immediately. However, Robert underwent double bypass heart surgery because his arteries were too small for the recommended triple bypass surgery.

Robert bounced back, and the following year he returned to his golf routine. Things seemed to be going well, but little did we know that round two was coming around the corner. It came extremely fast, and the wind and rain began to hit me hard once again. Within a short period of time we received the diagnosis that Robert had a very aggressive form of bone cancer, not to mention that a cancerous tumor was discovered on his lungs and was spreading to the other organs of his body. This caused rapid deterioration of his physical being.

This surely was not the way I expected my marriage to begin or what I thought marriage would be like. Truly, I knew that whatever God had for me, it was for me. After the first couple of years of my marriage, I was also broken from hurt and verbal abuse. I loved my husband, but when we had disagreements, it would require God to heal our marriage. God had to move. He saw that we were headed to a place of despair that filled our hearts and minds. Even though we would pray and even read or share Scripture together, only God could save us from the bitterness that was rising in our hearts. Faced with turmoil once again, I found myself wanting to run away from it all. I could not run away even though my mind said for me to run and keep moving. Where would I go? You can run. Where? "Oh, where can you turn?" said the adversary over and over. Here again, the "stinking thinking" was occurring, and I allowed it even though I knew better.

I stayed the course despite what friends and others said about our marriage. I was there, and I knew I had to stay. Sadly, after only four years marriage, Robert passed away. Now I was faced with another challenge and another blow and twist of my faith. Life was dealing me another challenge, one that would be even greater than the ones in the past. Through it all, God gave me the will power and called me to rise above everything I was going through. God was stretching His arms out to me while whispering in my ears how much He loved me and knew how my heart was hurting. From time to time—late at night when all was still and in the very early dawn of morning—my right ear would become empowered by a cooling sensation. God was speaking, and I just had to open my heart and let His voice be heard through my ears.

I reached a point in my life where I was experiencing an unusual feeling—this coolness—but I did not know what to do with it. Only with time did I realize that my spiritual maturity and awareness were developing, and this was God speaking to me. It was God whispering in my ears, my heart, and my mind: "You have the will power to rise above it. Use it!" When I first noticed this happening, I would try to shake the feeling. Yet, it grew stronger and more consistent like the waters that rose during the Flood. This coolness was empowering within me. Things were changing, I was changing, and God was changing the course of my life.

To describe this point of my life as anything other than a blessing would be 100 percent wrong. When I think about how I longed for peace and desired a better relationship with God, I had finally arrived there. I reached a place and point of knowing and accepting that

I had the will power and the call to rise above. My desire for this newness grew more, and God wanted more from me. He wanted more of my attention. God had already poured the foundation, the concrete of my being. Now, God was molding and shaping me for His divine purpose. Many days and nights, I was becoming overwhelmingly afraid of this feeling that I could not explain. Once again, as the many situations and trials of my past arose, I wanted to share this with someone. But with whom could I? My mother and husband had passed; and I did not think that my spiritual family at the time would understand. I did not even think that my pastor would understand where I was spiritually and where God was trying to take me.

The voice I heard was that of Jesus letting me know for sure that my destiny was burgeoning and forthcoming. I had not been here before, a place where I could hear the Lord's voice. God knew my heart and mind and wanted me to be in a place and position to communicate with Him more instead of other people. What a joy! It is an awesome feeling having God deposit His love and grace into our ears, heart, and mind. Finding daily peace and comfort from the pressure and discomfort I felt earlier in life gets me moving so much sometimes that I just have to stand and look at myself with pride.

God, who knows our hearts and very thoughts, reaches out with such a gentle touch; and everything seems to change. There was not a loud noise. It was soft, gentle, and peaceful. I knew something was happening, and it made me move into a better place. It gave me the peace I was longing for. I had to learn and teach myself to not fear the feeling but open my heart to the wonderful beauty and blessings God was instilling into my life. Despite what I knew and where my heart was, God was standing by my side; and I could hear His voice so clearly that it made my body leap. At other times, I allowed the adversary's voice to become louder and louder—so loud that it was all I could hear, and it seemed like all I knew.

First Peter 5:10-11 provides us with the decree that says: "After you have suffered for a little while, the God of all grace [who imparts His blessing and favor], who called you to His own eternal glory in Christ, will Himself complete, confirm, strengthen, and establish you [making you what you ought to be]. To Him be dominion (power, authority, sovereignty) forever and ever. Amen" (AMP). Truly, we all get there or have been there, as the saying goes, "Done that too!" What is important is how we get through the trials and the mess that we are in. Are we willing to stay in a place and time that continues to hurt us? Or are we going to push through, travailing like a woman fighting pains of labor, pushing with all she has to give birth? In the Gospel of John, Jesus declares unto the disciples:

> Verily, verily, I say unto you, That ye shall weep and lament, but the world shall rejoice: and ye shall be sorrowful, but your sorrow shall be turned into joy. A woman when she is in travail hath sorrow, because her hour is come: but as soon as she is delivered of the child, she remembereth no more the anguish, for joy that a man is born into the world. And ye now therefore have sorrow: but I will see you again, and your heart shall rejoice, and your joy no man taketh from you.
>
> JOHN 16:20-22

It is astonishing how when the rain falls so hard that all you can hear *is* the rain; and sometimes you hear nothing even though it could be falling and pounding hard on your rooftop. It is then that you lose the energy or strength to fight. If we can hear the gentle whisper of the Lord's voice calling to us, then we find the will power to rise above circumstances. Because of God's grace, compassion, and nature, we are victorious survivors. Of course, life will deal us some rough times, with these circumstances or situations being painful; but none of them could ever be as painful compared to what Jesus bore for you and me at Calvary. Jesus bore the greatest pain ever.

He went to Calvary and was beaten, whipped, laughed at, and dragged through the streets; yet He hung His head, bled, and died for us. What an awesome God we have and can truly rely on. Whether we are suffering something or not, Jesus is all we need.

Reflect now on how our Lord and Savior went to Calvary and think of a situation or circumstance that you have endured or faced which was painful—causing you to reflect and call on the name of Jesus. Absolutely, none could ever compare to the pain He bore. The pain Jesus bore is unimaginable for us to bear. He hung on the cross with sinners and never complained. Instead, He looked to His Father for help even though He could not always feel the presence of His Father. All of Jesus' suffering was foretold in the book of Isaiah.

> I gave my back to those who strike, and my cheeks to those who pull out the beard; I hid not my face from disgrace and spitting.
>
> ISAIAH 50:6 (ESV)

Jesus handled the devastation, tumult, and injustice of it all by trusting His Father. When He was reviled, He did not revile in return; when He suffered, He did not threaten but continued entrusting Himself to Him who judges justly.

Therefore doth my Father love me, because I lay down my life, that I might take it again. No man taketh it from me, but I lay it down of myself. I have power to lay it down, and I have power to take it again. This commandment have I received of my Father.

JOHN 10:17–18

Jesus did all for you and me; He was obedient. So why then do we complain when we go through even the smallest of things? Imagine being imprisoned for speaking the truth! It is written and guaranteed in the Bible that you will suffer persecution for the sake of being a follower of Christ.

Beloved, do not be surprised at the fiery trial when it comes upon you to test you, as though something strange were happening to you. But rejoice insofar as you share Christ's sufferings, that you may also rejoice and be glad when his glory is revealed. If you are insulted for the name of Christ, you are blessed, because the Spirit of glory and of God rests upon you. But let none of you suffer as a murderer or a thief or an evildoer or as a meddler. Yet if anyone suffers as a Christian, let him not be ashamed, but let him glorify God in that name. For it is time for judgment to begin at the household of God; and if it begins with us, what will be the outcome for those who do not obey the gospel of God? And "If the righteous is scarcely saved, what will become of the ungodly and the sinner?" Therefore let those who suffer according to God's will entrust their souls to a faithful Creator while doing good.

1 PETER 4:12-19 (ESV)

Yes, and all who desire to live godly in Christ Jesus will suffer persecution. But evil men and impostors will grow worse and worse, deceiving and being deceived. But you must continue in the things which you have learned and been assured of, knowing from whom you have learned them, and that from childhood you have known the Holy Scriptures, which are able to make you wise for salvation through faith which is in Christ Jesus. All Scripture is given by inspiration of God, and is profitable for doctrine, for reproof, for correction, for instruction in righteousness,

2 TIMOTHY 3:12-16 (NKJV)

Have you ever faced persecution for what you believe in or for speaking the truth about a matter? Have you ever waited a long time for something and it seemed like nothing was changing or God was not listening to your cries? Have you been waiting a long time for the promise of the Lord to be fulfilled in your life? Sure, you have. You must have grown weary, sad, and depressed — longing for answers. This, I believe, is God's way of taking us through tests and the proverbial changing of the seasons. It is all in God's divine plan for our life. Just as we endure the winter months—snow falling and cold temperatures—on the flip side there comes a season when everything seems so bright and colorful. With each changing season, God prepares us, supplying us with all we need to reach our destiny. Through it all, those that believe in Him and stand firm in His Word and love will prevail through whatever season they are currently in.

Oh, how wonderful it is to know that our heavenly Father reaches every point of our lives. He can heal the brokenhearted and will calm the storms, the wind, and the rain, causing it all to be still.

On that day, when evening came, Jesus said to his disciples, "Let's go across to the other side of the lake." So after leaving the crowd, they took him along, just as he was, in the boat, and other boats were with him. Now a great windstorm developed and the waves were breaking into the boat, so that the boat was nearly swamped. But he was in the stern, sleeping on a cushion. They woke him up and said to him, "Teacher, don't you care that we are about to die?" So he got up and rebuked the wind, and said to the sea, "Be quiet! Calm down!" Then the wind stopped, and it was dead calm. And he said to them, "Why are you cowardly? Do you still not have faith?"

They were overwhelmed by fear and said to one another, "Who then is this? Even the wind and sea obey
him!"

MARK 4:35-41 (NET)

FAMILY REUNION

Can you imagine yourself being in this situation? Well,
here I was, arriving at a time in life when I thought
things were really starting to get better. Mentally and
physically, my family seemed to be getting closer. I was
improving. I continued to pray for my family's restoration, as we had either drifted apart because of relocation
or because of the passing of a family member. My family
had grown smaller and smaller as the years passed by.
Bringing the family together was done especially for my
biological brother, LaMotte. LaMotte's future was in
jeopardy due to the terminal illness he had been suffering
from. At any rate, he had this illness in the past, but he
kept it to himself and his immediate family. LaMotte's
life was somewhat isolated, and only a few of our family
members even knew his wife and children—those being
the ones who actually attended their wedding. I knew
my brother's children because of my frequent visits with
them from time to time and occasional phone conversations. If you are wondering why my brother was not
mentioned until now, it is the result of how we grew up.

While growing up, we knew each other as cousins until another family secret was unveiled, or should I say discovered.

My family was embarrassed when anyone had children out of wedlock. To us it was a shameful thing. For many years throughout my childhood, I only knew of LaMotte as my distant cousin. However, Connie had given birth to two children out of wedlock: me and LaMotte. LaMotte was adopted by my aunt Sadie who lived in New York. Aunt Sadie's own biological son, Richie, had passed away; and she accepted LaMotte as her son. Richie fell from a tree at an early age, and the resulting trauma to his body was severe and devastating. Richie's passing was difficult for Aunt Sadie to accept. She cried and grieved for a long period of time. However, LaMotte was born shortly after Richie's death and taken in by Aunt Sadie.

LaMotte really enjoyed his life in New York. He attended school in New York and became gainfully employed in the years to come. As the years passed, I began to visit with Aunt Sadie and LaMotte in New York. I eventually relocated to New York after I graduated from high school in South Carolina. LaMotte and I shared few things together. There were a few times when our relationship had grown distant, but it was rekindled for a short while when Aunt Sadie became ill and passed away. Aunt Sadie was a fun-loving aunt. She would fight, speak whatever was on her mind, and keep moving. I remember the week before LaMotte was about to get married. She introduced me to his fiancée as LaMotte's sister, Pat. Well, no one took this seriously because Aunt Sadie was a known prankster. Shortly after LaMotte was married, an old friend named Helen came over to the house. LaMotte, Helen, and I were sitting around talking; and to our amazement Helen belted out, "Wow! You two sure look alike!" Our resemblance was astonishing, and years prior it had already been revealed to me in South Carolina that LaMotte was my biological brother, so I was not taken by surprise.

On one particular Saturday evening, some family friends came over to visit. Without reservation they blurted out, "Oh, you and your brother look so much alike. You both look like Connie." Oh my! Now another secret had been revealed, and I wondered if there were other secrets that would be let out of the bag.

As families in the North often sent their children to the South for the summer to visit relatives, prior to Aunt Sadie's passing LaMotte had a vacation that changed his life forever. During his time down south, he met a man whose name he didn't know, and all LaMotte told me was that this man kept telling him he looked like his mother, Connie. The fireworks began. LaMotte became rebellious and returned to New York, wanting to know what this man was talking about. Aunt Sadie confirmed the fact about who his real mother was, but LaMotte never accepted the fact that Connie was his biological mother. As for me, he consequently accepted me as his sister. However, we remained distant as the years passed, with only a casual phone call over the years.

Even though there was emotional distance between us, LaMotte and I often celebrated events of each other's accomplishments and that of other family members via our phone conversations. There were times when we talked, and I would talk about Jesus; but all he would do was say something sarcastic or just laugh. One day he actually asked me if I thought I was God, and my reply was that one day hopefully you will get to know Him as I do. Even though he might not have had the same perspective of God that I did, I still found Jesus to be the greatest friend of all. LaMotte later had a successful career in early childhood development and psychology for a community program in Boston until his illness. He assisted in many community development programs for families and was a great athlete during his college years at Villanova University.

Eventually, he passed away, and his passing was very difficult. After all, he was my biological brother. I had watched his health decline for a while and had gone to visit him before he passed. The last visit was excruciatingly painful as I witnessed his frail body lying there in the bed. He was a shell of his former self, and his body was now diminutive compared to how it had normally looked. He would turn his head as I spoke words to him, but I knew he could not see me. His eyes had turned bluish-grey, and his skin was now darker than ever. It was months later after this visit that I received a call informing me of my brother's passing. But God truly blessed him by allowing him to stay under hospice watch and walk out on his own in his right frame of mind with the ability to stand, eat, request dinner, and bathe himself. When the doctors gave up, even as family members gathered and chatted, God was still proving and showing us His power and magnificence.

HURRICANE TRAVAIL

I began to participate actively in church activities and Bible study, interceding in prayer for others. I prayed with others for their healing, deliverance, and weariness of life. I was getting involved again in community activities, and it was extremely refreshing. I felt I was in a good place spiritually, mentally, and physically.

In October 2014, I had several doctor visits during the year, and on one particular visit, I knew something was not so right. I felt the need to ask the doctor to order a mammogram for me. The doctor never questioned me but just sat in amazement and asked where I'd had the last one done. As I sat waiting on the nurse to return, fear began to surge in my mind; and in my heart I prayed that all would be well. As the days went by and the tests were ordered, reality set in. I was diagnosed with stage III breast cancer. Now, here I was feeling all alone as I began to reflect on how this same disease caused the death of my mother and grandmother. How was I going to tell my sons or anyone else? I wondered what people were going to say and think about me now. Questions galore kept racing frenetically through my mind! Notably, here again, the fear factor jumped right in and took a seat in my mind. The thought of being all alone and having no one to talk to—someone that would understand my condition—resonated within. Now, I believed I might have to face the criticism of people who only said negative things. To my amazement, as one goes through the fight of having cancer, people tend to not understand that it is not something we ask for; but it occurs, and we must battle for survival. So, why then do people ask the following types of questions: "Did you know you had cancer?" "Can you feel the lump?" "Does it hurt?" So, to avoid this, I simply held onto my situation and sought the kind of help that only God could give.

When the doctor read the report, I began to cry. I found myself really trying to hold back the tears, and I even apologized for crying. My inner being kept screaming, *Oh no, not me, not me*. In the midst of consoling me, the doctor assured me that I could get through this with the right treatments and surgery. I left the doctor's office that day, hurting and wondering how this could have happened. As I departed the cold, blue office, the lights appeared to be shining even brighter than before.

As the weeks went by and I began treatments, I witnessed several others going through the same condition, and I heard various testimonies of both struggle and triumph. Nothing made a difference until I met an angel in the treatment room one day. I was shocked that I could meet someone who really cared. Astoundingly, I believe as we go through life's journey, God does have a way of bringing a change to what appears to us as a great difficulty. I remember arriving for my first scheduled appointment, and I actually sat almost motionless. I did not know what to expect. I watched several others sitting and talking as their treatments were underway; and there were nurses busy giving injections and starting IVs. As the nurse approached me, she spoke and noted that I was sitting motionless; she wondered if I was okay. I assured her that I was fine, wishing she had not bothered me. I continued to stare deep into a nearby television to avoid any communication with anyone in the room. Seated and waiting in a chair next to me was a woman named Amanda. It just so happened that she would sit next to me every day I went for treatment. She reached out to me in my state of uneasiness, and we began to talk consistently during my treatments. I became fond of her presence and communication, and I looked forward to seeing her every day.

As time moved on and the treatments continued, I met many others; some I just watched, and others I chatted with about their treatments and recovery process. The effects of the treatments started to become noticeable as I began to lose most of my appetite and become fatigued. On one Saturday night as I was preparing for the following day's church service by rolling my hair up, the curlers from my hair began to unravel, one by one, and my tiny curls dissipated. I looked, only to notice that the tiny curls, all neatly rolled, had fallen to the floor, leaving me almost bald. Ironically, I did not feel any fear; I just wanted to cry, and a few tears began to fall from my eyes. I continued to stare in the mirror and unroll each curl. My mind was made up, and I accepted the fact that there was nothing I could do about my hair loss. Within an instant I rationalized that wigs would be the only option at my disposal. To my advantage, I occasionally wore wigs, so no one really saw or noticed my baldness. Yet, lingering in my mind were the visions of many women I'd seen in the treatment center wearing scarfs wrapped tightly around their heads. I was prepared to move on and do whatever was necessary to survive. Hair, I thought, would just grow back over time!

On one particular visit to the doctor's office, I had become so weak that the nurse wheeled me in a wheelchair to a nearby waiting car. I was so weak that even the driver and the attending nurse wondered if I was okay. Through the divine love of God, I gained the strength I needed to return home to rest for the day. Truthfully, I was wondering as to how and if I was ever going to recover at that age. Here is without a doubt proof that God is real and loves those who believe and trust in Him. Meeting the people that I did as the weeks went by sincerely helped me get through. Help was present throughout the duration of my treatments and surgery. I thought I would not be able to share my pain, thoughts, fears, and emotional or physical hurt. I was more afraid of the reactions that I thought I would receive from friends and even some family members. God placed several people around me that I could trust and share my circumstances with and that understood what I was going through. I did not worry about the confidentiality because the few individuals that I did share my circumstances with, undoubtingly and faithfully prayed and fasted, believing God for healing in the weeks and months of treatment prior to surgery.

> And this is the confidence that we have toward him, that if we ask anything according to his will he hears us. And if we know that he hears us in whatever we ask, we know that we have the requests that we have asked of him.
>
> 1 JOHN 5:14-15 (ESV)

As the treatments came to an end and the doctors prepared me for surgery, God performed a miracle in my body. At the time of my diagnosis, the doctor was mystified by what he saw. To the amazement of the doctors, they unhesitatingly called a meeting with a radiologist, surgeon, pathologist and anesthesiologist. Together, they looked at the lab work and x-rays, discussing the appropriate surgical method. Previously, all the x-rays showed that there was a tumor present. However, none of the tests revealed where the cancer or the tumor had originated. The tumor and cancer rested in one area; and in total disbelief, the doctors continued to order test after test, scans, and imaging. However, no further developments were detected. They were searching for something that could not be found. Visually, all that could be found was a branch with no limbs or tree trunk to hang from. I had a branch with no leaves, no trunk, and no sign of existing object attached to it. I met with the oncologist weeks after the team had their meeting, and as I sat in the cold waiting room, I remembered what my mother had gone through. Afraid to tell anyone of her condition, she hid it from everyone, including myself, until it was obvious that she needed immediate medical treatment.

Still in amazement, the doctors could not understand why the x-rays did not show anything as they described this foreign item in my body as something unique with no tree trunk and just a hanging branch suspended in my body. Various tests could not reveal what the doctors hoped to find. I knew then, despite my diagnosis, that God was at work and nothing else mattered. God was still in control of my wellbeing; and no matter what the medical reports said, God was showing them He had the situation in His hand. Exodus 15:26 pronounces: "...If you will diligently listen to the voice of the LORD your God, and do that which is right in his eyes, and give ear to his commandments and keep all his statutes, I will put none of the diseases on you that I put on the Egyptians, for I am the LORD, your healer" (ESV). The Lord God clearly had plans for my life, future, and destiny.

The morning of surgery arrived. A dear confidant arrived, escorted me to the hospital, and was my support throughout the day. As the nurses prepped me, the reality check of the surgery began to stare me right in the face. I seemed to have run out of smiles; no more smiles or tears for now. I felt in my heart that all would be well, though my outer appearance was displaying something different. As I began to stare and gaze around in the bright green, shaded room, there stood a tall, distinguished nurse watching me. The nurse began to approach me. As she drew closer and closer to me, I could see a reassuring and consoling look donning her face. She softly whispered to me that she was a thirteen-year breast cancer survivor. Before she turned and walked away, she smilingly whispered that I should let her know if I needed anything.

God was there all the time and was letting me know He was right by my side. My eyes were busy looking everywhere. My vision was cloudy; and I was looking and staring in all the wrong places—sideways, at the walls and down at the floor. However, He was there, and all I needed to do was just lift my head.

The earth is the Lord's, and the fulness thereof; the world, and they that dwell therein. For he hath founded it upon the seas, and established it upon the floods. Who shall ascend into the hill of the Lord? or who shall stand in his holy place? He that hath clean hands, and a pure heart; who hath not lifted up his soul unto vanity, nor sworn deceitfully. He shall receive the blessing from the Lord, and righteousness from the God of his salvation. This is the generation of them that seek him, that seek thy face, O Jacob. Selah. Lift up your heads, O ye gates; and be ye lift up, ye everlasting doors; and the King of glory shall come in. Who is this King of glory? The Lord strong and mighty, the Lord mighty in battle. Lift up your heads, O ye gates; even lift them up, ye everlasting doors; and the King of glory shall come in. Who is this King of glory? The Lord of hosts, he is the King of glory. Selah.

PSALM 24:1-10

I thought to myself that it was time for me to stop trying to fix things and let God do His work in me. I was not functioning on my own, but it was the love of God that continued to flow through me; and this is why I had the capability to live. Funny thing, people confess to being a child of the King, saved, and filled with the Holy Ghost but forget the promises of the Lord. God gives strength and the wisdom to overcome to those whom believe, trust, and obey Him.

Another nurse arrived, this one assisting me to the restroom. She noticed my constant shaking and immediately began to hold on to me. I had no clue I was that nervous and shaky. I was in panic mode again. Deeply seeded fear lingered in me and began to swell. Shortly thereafter, with my confidant still by my side and in deep meditation, I was given a sedative; and all I could hear was the sound of the squeaking wheels on the bed as I was rolled toward the surgery room. My confidant stood and whispered a prayer to me, assuring me that I would be fine.

The doors to the surgical room swung open as the nurse touched the keypad on the wall; and minutes later I was met by the surgical team. With my eyes gazing around, I looked at the various instruments, bright lights, and people standing in the corner talking—pondering the notion that one way or another my life would be changed shortly. As I looked around the room, a very long, stern-looking face told me that she was going to give me additional medication and help me turn on my side. I asked where the doctor was and joked about a previous surgery in which the medical team and I laughed about me being hungry and wanting Chinese food just before the procedure. As I lay on my side, I thought, *Wow this is really going to happen.* It is about to be on now. Stirring in the back of my mind were thoughts both troublesome and good. I thank God that His love for me is so marvelous. As I continued to look around the room, I began to pray. I found myself saying Matthew 6:9-13: "Our Father which art in heaven, Hallowed be thy name. Thy kingdom come. Thy will be done in earth, as it is in heaven. Give us this day our daily bread. And forgive us our debts, as we forgive our debtors. And lead us not into temptation, but deliver us from evil: For thine is the kingdom, and the power, and the glory, forever. Amen."

As preparation time was in full force, I was given instruction to remain in position; and with the assistance of the nearby medical team, I was turned to my side. As with previous surgeries, I thought, *Okay I will just chat with them until they ask me to count backward*. Ha ha! Shockingly, after questioning where the surgeon was, I found myself waking up in the recovery room hours later. What a mighty and awesome God we serve! As He guided me through, He held my hand and loved me despite me not totally surrendering everything to Him.

Here again, my faith was tested, as I was contrarily looking for the presence of an earthly man. My hope and love for God grew even stronger, and as the days passed, my recovery was well underway. Upon being rolled from the recovery suite into my assigned room, there stood friends and family members waiting and celebrating my successful surgery. Even then, it did not feel as though I had just come out of surgery. The expectation of those waiting was that I would be sedated and sleepy. Not me! I was wide awake. I was free from what was trying to attack me physically and mentally. I was free because of the marvelous healing that God had performed in my body. I was free because I love the Lord, and he loves me as His daughter. Thank God, I was free from the thought of having cancer spread throughout my body. I am free! Glory to God my healer, deliverer, and comforter. I am free.

The doctors arrived to speak with me about post-surgery procedures. Astonishingly, everyone looking at me seemed a bit stunned, noting that I looked so much younger and now had a brighter complexion. This was my healer working miracles and showing He is God almighty. God was proving Himself so that I would believe and help others to believe. God will and can do things that mankind can only dream of and imagine doing themselves.

> For wisdom will enter your heart, and knowledge will
> be pleasant to your soul. Discretion will protect you,
> and understanding will guard you.
>
> PROVERBS 2:10-11 (NIV)

I began another round of radiation treatment to destroy any cells that may have lingered around in my breast after surgery. The doctors assured me that the surgery was successful, and the cancerous tumor had been removed. In all the excitement of the success, it was also noted that I had stage II breast cancer rather than the previously diagnosed stage III. Glory be to God for this marvelous and wonderful blessing. I reached a point where nothing could impede my declaration of loving the Lord even more. In Psalm 103, David says: "Bless the Lord O my soul: and all that is within me bless His holy name. Bless the Lord, O my soul, and forget not all His benefits: Who forgiveth all thine iniquities; who healeth all thy diseases; Who redeemed thy life from destruction; who crowneth thee with loving-kindness and tender mercies; Who satisfieth thy mouth with good things; so that thy youth is renewed like the eagle's" (vv. 1-5). I declare that I will bless the Lord always; and although struggles and trials may continue to come, through it all, my soul shall continue to praise God because He is my keeper, my healer, and my deliverer. He truly brought me through. I wanted so desperately to tell someone my story; but the fear of what they might say or how they might treat me remained heavy in my heart and mind. I could almost hear the voices, and I could imagine the laughter of those people in my mind. I imagined the chatter that would take place, in addition to the sneering faces. I began to imagine that only a few would take me seriously. I imagined that many would have a pity party as though I had something contagious, something that I could pass on through a tissue or handkerchief which I had sneezed on. Shortly thereafter, I was able to continue my community and church related activities.

A year after my initial diagnosis, I found myself participating in a tribute program that was dedicated to individuals who were either battling or had overcome breast cancer. As I witnessed the various testimonies from the breast cancer survivors, I wanted to say, "Here I am. I am a survivor! Look at me! I am healed, and I have a new outlook on life. God loves me so much that He performed a true miracle." Thus, being fearful and convinced that I would be laughed at, talked about, and stared at for days to come, I made every effort to keep quiet and appear normal. Some people said that I was a little out of character. That is putting it nicely. Given the fact that I had such a secret, I will admit that I did not appear as myself. I did apologize to anyone who thought of me as being indifferent. But know that God is still working in me. I am working on developing into a Kingdom builder and warrior for Christ. Having the ability to grow, we become like leaves falling from the trees and getting trampled on the ground. I have plenty of room for improvement, but I also have an earnest desire to be who God has called me to be.

The heartaches and negative thought process became my daily medicine once again. It almost seemed to be my daily vitamin. Speaking of which, during my treatments—thank God for speaking to me and giving me the discerning spirit to know it was Him speaking—God whispered to me and advised me to take vitamin C daily; and I still take one tablet daily. Vitamin C in pill form and the Word of God in daily doses brought me through each day and night, and it remains this way now. God was not giving up on me, and surely, I will not give up on Him. I desire God to speak to my mind and heart daily and to lead me to a place called T.H.R.O.U.G.H.

Here I was, standing high upon what seemed like a mountain. I can only imagine how Moses felt on the mountain when he spoke to the Lord and received instructions. High above my circumstances, I had to rise above it all. It was God's gift to bless me with the will power and call to rise above situations while preparing me for greater days and years ahead.

THE WHOLE WORLD IN HIS HANDS

Even after I had experienced a miracle in my health and received the gift of life, the negative thinking was becoming very strong again. I was truly struggling and straining to keep my focus on the things I had learned through my past experiences. Through the obvious negative thinking and the tricks of the adversary, at this point I began to see clouds—clouds bigger, brighter, and sometimes stretching wider and wider across the blue sky. I felt the wind blowing from the south to the north and from the east to the west. The winds were blowing, pushing, tossing, and shifting things. Here it was, another twist and another chapter set to be written. My life, character, and all that I had experienced in my life from birth to the present time were turning around. As the wind blew, the sweet whispers of the Lord were there, and He spoke louder each time. It was time to move away from the point of destruction, hurt, shame, and despair. My heavenly Father desired for me to get up because He had already paved the road. Headed down Destruction Avenue, which in turn would lead to Failure Boulevard, I was not able to realize that I was free or that I just needed to pick myself up, get my act together, and not allow the adversary to lead me down this deserted path anymore. I could no longer stay; and I did not belong there.

"I have declared the former things from the beginning; They went forth from My mouth, and I caused them to hear it. Suddenly I did them, and they came to pass.

ISAIAH 48:3 (NKJV)

The storm was now over; and I was preparing to move forward for greater works and abundant life. God healed my body and began to show me how to renew my mind as well. Renewing my mind would free me from the negative thinking and allow me to focus more on resting and relying on His promises. As I began to look back over my life, I began to reflect on how I often found myself on an emotional roller coaster. My emotions became so frantic that nothing made any sense anymore. The choice was obvious, and I chose to praise God in the singing voices of the angels that I clearly heard in my ears. Now, God began a new thing in me because I trusted and believed in Him. The realization of His doing what He said He would do was in sight. God was teaching me that I was not in control of my destiny but that He was. He controlled my path and my direction. God declares in Scripture, "I am Alpha and Omega, the beginning and the ending, saith the Lord, which is, and which was, and which is to come, the Almighty" (Revelation 1:8).

I realized and accepted that God was in control and the storm had passed over. The realization of my newfound hope gave birth and new meaning to who I am. I realized that I am the daughter of the great King and Ruler and had to let Him be God in my life. Accepting

Christ as my Redeemer was significant to the future of my life's journey.

Far too many times we cry out to the Lord when in distress or pain and when we seek directions. This is a good practice; but when God brings us through the storm, tests, trials, and tribulations, we oftentimes kick Him to the curb. This should not be, but we do it nonetheless. Yet, God, being who He is, embraces us with arms wide open and loves us even more. Seeking God makes the difference, and it is imperative that we learn to remain above situations and circumstances that make us doubt, fear, and try to fix things ourselves. I am guilty of all of the above. I wanted to do many things my way. In retrospect, I now realize that it's not about my way. Even though I might be experiencing a new day and new direction in life, it is and always will be all about God's way. This is the choice I had to make if I wanted to live life to its fullest potential.

Was I staying in God's way when I tried to fix things my way? Of course not! My mind said one thing, and my heart cried something else. Here is the true meaning of "amazing grace." Here I was blind, and I just could not see through life's misty rain or fog. Although I knew in my heart where the answers and resolution resided— trusting, hoping and believing in God—the rebirthing had to be initiated within me. What a loving father God is! He is someone who is always there by our side, even through life's challenges. Yet, all He wants is for us to believe, trust, and obey Him. He sacrificed so much for us so that we can walk, talk, eat, sleep, and live freely. In spite of His goodwill toward us, many still manage to struggle finding time to praise God and glorify Him.

To my amazement, learning how to be obedient through life's storms helped in the renewal of my thinking, as would the way I handled the situations and circumstances in the days, months, and years to follow. The coolness and emptiness I once felt had now morphed into something so proliferating and invigorating that I felt the need to tell someone. I wanted to help someone else. I was seeking something now more than ever. I wanted to give birth to what was burgeoning on the inside of me! Here's where the labor pains grew more and more, and contractions began to push harder and stronger than before. My stomach and total posture were different. The contractions were forcing me to open my spirit and heart to becoming who I was meant to be. There came this impulse of hope and willingness to fight for the things that I had previously been robbed of. I was willing to fight for the many things that I doubted would happen and for the care of others. Nothing mattered because God was using me and giving me strength like never before; and I was gaining power I never imagined I could have.

Earlier in my life, my mother Connie would always tell me that I had great faith, but I would just scoff at her remark and laugh it off in nonchalance. Connie would just look at me; but now I realize that in her heart and mind she was praying and seeking God on my behalf. My mother, grandmother Nora, Aunt Pat, and Connie have all passed on now; yet, I know without a doubt that all of them labored in tear-drenched prayer on many a night, all with the intention of me having a relationship with God.

So, where was I, who was I, and who am I? I asked myself this, as I had to come to grips with myself. Finally, I realized that I had a true calling to rise above. I had already won, but because I was blind, I could not see the will power and for a long time ignored the call of God to rise up even though it was instilled deep down inside of me. The load I carried—which most of us do unnecessarily—was already lifted at Calvary. The blood of Jesus paid the price for our freedom. Somehow, I often found myself feeling trapped, but taking the proper stance at this point on would determine who I would become. I had to learn how to renew my mind with the Word of God because we are transformed when we renew our minds and our ways.

> Do not conform to the pattern of this world, but be transformed by the renewing of your mind. Then you will be able to test and approve what God's will is—his good, pleasing and perfect will.
>
> ROMANS 12:2 (NIV)

We have God's promise, and His name is Jesus! Oh, how wonderful it is to know Him. Receive Him into your hearts and minds, praise Him, and praise Him through whatever you go through. God gave me strength that I never saw coming. I was no longer shattered by many of the challenges I faced and endured. Going through was rough, and it became so hard that I wanted to quit. I often lacked the energy I needed to fight on. Nevertheless, God was and still is working in and through me. I became confident as I awaited greater blessings from the Lord, but the adversary knew God's plan of leading me, guiding me, and holding my hand throughout my life's journey. The enemy's attacks became harder to bear; but my God is still alive, and He reigns forevermore. God has not given up on me. What I discovered was that I had to fight with everything that I knew, had learned, and was taught. Everything that God had birthed in me was what

I had to use to fight the battle with; and I had to trust, have faith, and believe that God would grant me victory.

> I have said these things to you, that in me you may have peace. In the world you will have tribulation. But take heart; I have overcome the world."
>
> JOHN 16:33 (ESV)

Moreover, in everything that we go through in life, God can get us through. He can calm any sea, high tides, or water overflow. Think now of the high tides that have pushed you and caused you pain, sorrow, and even shame. Since God is in the heavens, and He is above the situation and the waters, there is no need for us to hold our heads down when the tide seems to be rising well above our heads. Look up to the heavens and declare Him as King, Lord, God, and Savior.

> I will lift up mine eyes unto the hills, from whence cometh my help. My help cometh from the Lord, which made heaven and earth. He will not suffer thy foot to be moved: he that keepeth thee will not slumber. Behold, he that keepeth Israel shall neither slumber nor sleep.
>
> PSALM 121:1-4

The biblical story of Jonah, who was swallowed and trapped in the belly of a whale, suggests to us that even when we're in situations that are hopeless, we can find within us the strength and power to cry out to the Lord.

> Saying, "I called out to the LORD, out of my distress, and he answered me; out of the belly of Sheol I cried, and you heard my voice. For you cast me into the deep, into the heart of the seas, and the flood surrounded me; all your waves and your billows passed over me. Then I said, 'I am driven away from your sight; yet I shall again look upon your holy temple.' The waters closed in over me to take my life; the deep surrounded me; weeds were wrapped about my head at the roots of the mountains. I went down to the land whose bars closed upon me forever; yet you brought up my life from the pit, O LORD my God. When my life was fainting away I remembered the LORD, and my prayer came to you, into your holy temple.
>
> JONAH 2:2-7 (ESV)

Making it a practice to look up to the true and only source of our being paves and imprints our paths to reach for greater heights and strength in our Christian journey and in life in general. First John 4:4 declares, "You are of God, little children, and have overcome them, because He who is in you is greater than he who is in the world." It is in our determination and willingness to press forward that we garner the strength to overcome and triumph over any obstacle we encounter.

As I reflect on my daily trips for treatments and doctor visits, I am reminded of how I stared out of the car window as the cars passed by and moved swiftly on the highway. I was mesmerized by Broad River, the large body of water that I crossed over en route to the treatment center. I had traveled this route many times before the cancer treatments, but it had never held my attention in such a way. It was raining on most days I traveled to the doctor's office; and as I looked across the bridge from side to side, gazing as far as I could see into the waters across the bridge, the thought of Creation popped in my mind. I began to think about the Biblical account of Creation in the book of Genesis.

In the beginning, God created the heavens and the earth. The earth was without form and void, and darkness was over the face of the deep. And the Spirit of God was hovering over the face of the waters. And God said, 'Let there be light,' and there was light, and God saw that the light was good. And God separated the light from the darkness. God called the light day, and the darkness He called night. And there was evening and there was morning, the first day. And God said, 'Let there be an expanse in the midst of the waters, and let it separate the waters from the waters.' And God made the expanse and separated the waters that were under the expanse from the waters that were above the expanse. And it was so. And God called the expanse Heaven. And there was evening and there was morning, the second day. And God said, 'Let the waters under the heavens be gathered together into one place, and let the dry land appear.' And it was so. God called the dry land Earth, and the waters that were gathered together called Seas. And saw that it was good. And God said, 'Let the earth sprout vegetation, plants yielding seed, and fruit trees bearing fruit in which is their seed, each according to its kind, on the earth.' And it was so. The earth brought forth vegetation, plants yielding seed according to their own kinds, and trees bearing fruit in which is their seed, each according to its kind. And God saw that it was good. And there was evening and there was morning, the third day. And God said, 'Let there be lights in the expanse of the heavens to separate the day from the night. And let them be for signs and for seasons, and for days and years, and let them be lights in the expanse of the heavens to give light upon the earth.' And it was so. And God made the two great lights the greater light to rule the day and the lesser light to rule the night and the stars. And God set them in the expanse of the heavens to give light on the earth, to rule over the day and over the night, and to separate the light from the darkness. And God saw that it was good. And there was evening and there was morning, the fourth day. And God said, 'Let the waters swarm with swarms of living creatures, and let birds fly above the earth across the expanse of the heavens.' So, God created the great sea creatures and every living creature that moves, with which the waters swarm, according to their kinds, and every winged bird according to its kind. And God saw that it was good. And God blessed them, saying, 'Be fruitful and multiply and fill the waters in the seas, and let birds multiply on the earth.' And there was evening and there was morning, the fifth day. And God said, 'Let the earth bring forth living creatures according to their kinds — livestock and creeping things and beasts of the earth according to their kinds.' And it was so. And God made the beasts of the earth according to their kinds and the livestock according to their kinds, and everything that creeps on the ground according to its kind. And God saw that it was good.

GENESIS 1:1-25 (ESV)

It never seemed to be a heavy downpour of rain a majority of the days that I went for treatments. To my amazement I found myself looking as far as I could see across the waters. I became fascinated with the tall trees that I viewed, and the thought of the earth being empty at the time of Creation had become a part of my imagination. On one particular day while traveling across the bridge, it was extremely foggy; and the rain was pouring down heavily. The sky was gray, and only a few clouds were visible. My thoughts and my sight became enthralled by the trees and the fog that were visible across the waters. There were no visible waves in the water, and everything appeared tranquil and still. I began to imagine what it must have been like when the earth was formed out of darkness and stillness. In the days that followed, I continued imagining what each day of the Creation, the beginning of time, and the existence of Adam and Eve were like. Lingering in my thoughts was how blessed I was despite what I'd been going through. I still had life and the promise of the Lord that He would supply my needs just as He provided everything for Adam and Eve.

> But my God shall supply all your need according to his riches in glory by Christ Jesus.
>
> PHILIPPIANS 4:19

As I journeyed each day across the bridge, I not only thought about Creation, but it was at the forefront of my view now. I saw the earth being void and empty, full of darkness. I began to see God's gift of life to mankind and His provision of everything we could or would ever need for existence. I had never been so moved by the view of the trees and the water until now. As I continued daily to look across the water, the thought remained in my mind that God loves us very much.

Determined and making every possible attempt to turn me around, Satan continued his efforts to distract me. Praise the Lord, for He remained by my side, watching on as Satan played his tricks on me. I am so thankful to God that only He has my future in His hands. God's plans are greater, and they have manifested to shed light upon my life. I just had to get T.H.R.O.U.G.H. by going through.

> For the vision is yet for an appointed time, but at the end it shall speak, and not lie: though it tarry, wait for it; because it will surely come, it will not tarry.
>
> HABAKKUK 2:3

Thus far, my life has been an unforgettable and remarkable journey. I will forever be grateful to God for allowing me to reach this point. In the past there were times when I just sat and watched the seasons change, wondering what was next. I would frequently stare at the various flowers blooming in my yard or just find myself lying in bed and listening to the birds chirping away in my window every morning, singing their song of praise. All of these occurrences of nature are reminders of God's love. Ultimately, I changed, as did my thoughts and inner being that once pondered if a blue sky actually existed. God saw and knew in the beginning of my life, before my conception, that I would overcome the many hurdles, ups and downs, trials, tests, and experiences that I had to go through. I believe that He just needed me to believe and trust in Him wholeheartedly.

> My son forget not my law; but let thine heart keep my commandments: For length of days, and long life, and peace, shall they add to thee. Let not mercy and truth forsake thee: bind them about thy neck; write them upon the table of thine heart: So shalt thou find favour and good understanding in the sight of God and man. Trust in the LORD with all thine heart; and lean not unto thine own understanding In all thy ways acknowledge him, and he shall direct thy paths. Be not wise in thine own eyes: fear the LORD, and depart from evil. It shall be health to thy navel, and marrow to thy bones.
>
> PROVERBS 3:1-8

Through the maturation process, I would learn how to believe in God to do all that I needed. I am nothing without Him in my life. I arrived at the point where I am in life now by knowing that there is nothing like the love of the Lord God.

(T)EMPORARY:
THE MISSION BEGINS

———— - ————

L ife is amazing. It is wonderful, full of joy, but at the same time has its presence of heartache, shame, and pain. Life, as we have it, is a place called T.H.R.O.U.G.H.—a temporary holding place of isolation. However, through it all, life offers us the opportunity to grow, learn, and mature. I understand now that my life has been ordained, and that it was God's divine will for me to arrive at my present state, place, and time.

I was no longer to be held back in a place of standing still; something was destined to come forth. I suffered and endured the toughest of times, times in which I was always limiting myself due to lack of understanding of my real purpose and what I was to do in life. I reached a point where I thought that everything would change, and I would no longer have to suffer through things. However, I had to go through in order to reach a point of understanding and be able to give back to others who were going through as well.

Disappointment after disappointment, no matter what happened I was still standing at the same station. It felt as if my life had been designed in such a way that many would classify it as meaningless. But God, who saw and allowed me to go through this state, was grooming me both in the physical and mental. I was held down and let down mentally and physically. Mentally, I only saw despair, displacement, and discomfort. Transition was not a thing in my life, or so I thought. On the other hand, I was wrong to think that I was not moving from one place to another. God had His hands all over my life and being. I was in a temporary state of being, just walking and strolling along Temporary Boulevard. However, Jesus was with me every step of the way. My steps were already ordained by God, and I just had to travel the ordained path.

Life has its moments; there were moments when I felt like nothing mattered. I had heard of a man called Jesus—a wonderful King who reigned forever—but I was so blindsided by my misery that I did not have an understanding or clear vision of who Jesus is. Spiritually, I was lost, although not forever. I just had to find a way to get out. I had to grip onto something and someone to move me from what seemed to be a permanent state of existence. This *was* not and *is* not who I am because the Bible tells me that greater is He that is in me than he that is in the world (1 John 4:4). Jesus lives within me; and I live because of Him.

The turbulence, wind, and rain that constantly blew my way were only temporary. I had to learn denial and how not to accept the bleakness of my life. Here's where "temporary" meant always growing from doing nothing and accepting everything as it was. I saw myself wading knee-deep in water that I would drown in if I had not seen the true light shining upon my life. My cure was nothing temporary; it was a permanent design. It was the birth of the new me, the gift that hid so very deep within me. Call it what you want, but I know it as the will power and the true calling to rise above. Glory! Glory be to God for His goodness in everything I've been through despite disobedience, ignorance, and me giving the adversary the will to control my mind. It was my calling to rise through the mud and sinking sand along the road I had been traveling. It happened very quickly and shortly. The pre-operational state for my destiny, my purpose and answering my calling to be a servant of the Lord would help me elevate from my "temporary" state.

God's will is that we live, whereas the evil being and his cohorts seek to destroy us by distracting and taking us away from whom God designed and intended for us to be. Through examination of myself, something I find myself often doing a lot, I can now see my true image. I am the child of the Highest and the only true God. I am the daughter of the King, who reigns forever. I belong to Him, and He is my source of being. Hallelujah! Glory to the Lord. I found hope, peace, and joy. I know who I am. I no longer doubt myself or my journey. There is no doubt that I can do all things through Christ who strengthens me (Philippians 4:13).

I had to arrive at a place in my thinking and belief where I truly believed in myself and what God was doing in me. I had to see the vision God had for me; and I had to focus on my walk, talk, and actions. I was so focused on what was not working and the things that kept coming to distract me from my destiny that I did not realize a lot of my struggles were my fault. I had allowed the devil to distract me time after time. What I was not doing was listening to the voice of the Lord, even though it was speaking so clearly and loudly in my heart and mind. The enemy was playing games with my mind; he was up to his usual tricks, and I was his target. But thank God, for He was standing in my path and waiting for me to realize the gift that I had; and that gift was will power.

Although T.H.R.O.U.G.H just seemed like impossibility at the time, it was very much possible; but it was my belief that would make all the difference. Where was my hope? Where was my vision? Had I lost all that God birthed inside of me? No, I just became sidetracked, and God allowed me to go through because He needed and wanted me to reach out to Him more and more every day. The first stage of getting T.H.R.O.U.G.H was just temporary, and it was not my final destination. On the other hand, this first step of journeying toward T.H.R.O.U.G.H was significant to the sum total of my life. I was already a winner, and I was victorious. Nothing or no one could claim my victory other than Jesus Himself, seated on the heavenly throne with His Father.

Now, here I am, no longer questioning what to do or who to turn to. Life has a new meaning, and I am now able to see the rainbow. Clearly, I can see that I do have a purpose in life. Of course, I know the devil will continue to try me in every way, but I have also learned how to apply my will power and how to use this gift to rise above every attack of the devil. There is no more isolation, and no more being captive or held back from the things God desired for my life. I have traveled a different path now. I have will power, and yes, I am determined every day to rise above all that had caused the deterrence in the journey to my destiny.

I remember my mother's prayer life and how she would simply pray all day—no television, radio, or outside distractions, just she and Jesus Christ communicating night and day. Nothing would get to her until change came and she was sure God had heard her prayer. Even in her illness and state of declining health, she put her face down, bent her knees, and looked up to heaven; she did this daily. As the days and weeks passed, I continuously watched her, often wondering how she did it. Little did I know that God was using this situation to help define me; and now, here I am, standing as tall as the trees. I am T.H.R.O.U.G.H., having learned from my mother how to pray, even when I tried to ignore her presence and sometimes her teachings. Today, and only by the grace and love of God, I am standing firm on the promises of the Lord. No matter what the circumstance, here I am. Temporary is no longer center stage. It was in the past, and I am moving forward, living life as it has been ordained. I am blessed, and everyone that trusts and believes in God can be blessed too. Let the promises of God not only be in your thoughts but show up in your actions, speech, and daily living. Celebrate Jesus. Celebrate the victory that He's won for us on Calvary, for in Him we have the victory and are winners!

> For by grace are ye saved through faith; and that not of yourselves: it is the gift of God:
>
> EPHESIANS 2:8

Hallelujah! Hallelujah! Hallelujah! Thank you, Jesus, for saving me is my song of praise. No more temporary holding places, self-rejection, or running away from the voice of the Lord. Temporary places and people have all become a thing of the past. The temporary season is over. It is over! Getting through was always harder than the previous time. It was hard. My journey seemed bleaker and bleaker, and nothing was making sense. Almost to a point of crying continually, I became desperate for help. Glory be to God, for my help was right by my side. I was like the man who waited by the pool of Bethesda for help. I was hurting so much that I needed and wanted to be healed. Yes, I laid awake many nights and sat silently during most days, just staring out of the window and looking for a ray of hope and peace. Nothing was happening for me. Be that as it may, darkness was everywhere, even within all of my thoughts; and I just wanted someone to do something quick.

Going back to the impotent man at the pool of Bethesda, he had been there poolside for thirty-eight years, waiting daily for someone to put him in the pool. He had lost the use of his limbs, at least on one side. God knew and saw his struggle, determination, and belief that he would be healed if he could only reach the pool. Here comes Jesus, who called upon the impotent man to rise up and walk. The man adhered to the word of the Lord, and immediately his limbs were quickened. He got up and walked.

> After this there was a feast of the Jews, and Jesus went up to Jerusalem. Now there is in Jerusalem by the Sheep Gate a pool, which is called in Hebrew, Bethesda, having five porches. In these lay a great multitude of sick people, blind, lame, paralyzed, waiting for the moving of the water. For an angel went down at a certain time into the pool and stirred up the water; then whoever stepped in first, after the stirring of the water, was made well of whatever disease he had. Now a certain man was there who had an infirmity thirty-eight years. When Jesus saw him lying there, and knew that he already had been in that condition a long time, He said to him, "Do you want to be made well?" The sick man answered Him, "Sir, I have no man to put me into the pool when the water is stirred up; but while I am coming, another steps down before me." Jesus said to him, "Rise, take up your bed and walk."

And immediately the man was made well, took up his bed, and walked.

JOHN 5:1-9 (NKJV)

Here I was, waiting and wanting to be healed; but due to doubt and the enemy's tricks, my faith was tested over and over again. Thank God for giving me a chance to hear His voice; and He called me to rise above the pain I was feeling. He urged me to rise up above my circumstances and move forward. He was with me the entire time—waiting, ready, and willing to heal me.

Healing will occur as we learn to open our hearts and seek God as our healer instead of trying to be our own healer. The impotent man wanted to be healed, and he had to patiently watch as others were being healed on a daily basis. Despite this, he continued to believe that if he could only get in the pool he would be alright. He too struggled to get through, and he struggled over and over to be in the waters of healing. Wherein, he too could have just given up and turned around on his destiny, healing, and time of deliverance; but something persistent was teeming inside of him.

God had a plan for this man, and He has a plan for you and me too. Psalm 34:17 says, "When the righteous cry for help, the Lord hears and delivers them out of all their troubles" (ESV). If you will just reach out to God,

He will take notice of your plea and answer you. God is the ultimate deliverer and will never turn a blind eye or deaf ear to His children.

On one particular occasion some time back, I was invited to travel to Ecuador with a friend on a mission trip. The goal was to help establish and set up churches. I was excited and looked forward to the venture so much that I even began to collect Bibles and literature for the trip. During my senior year of high school, I remember our guidance counselor asking the senior class what our career goals were. At the time, I wanted to be the next Barbara Walters, traveling and exploring different parts of the world. I'd hoped to become a journalist as I would get to tell stories of struggles and challenges of people across the world to a viewing audience. To be honest, I thought I would replace Barbara Walters as a reporter. Seriously, I really thought that *I* was the one! While most of my friends and family members would watch their favorite television shows or movies, I always loved watching the news. I was never content until I had watched the morning and evening news broadcasts.

Due to another health challenge, I was unable to go on the mission trip. I had developed arthritis in my knees, and so I required surgery. Health challenges seemed to follow me, yet thank God that survival came my way. It was in my DNA. God did not let me down. He continued to carry me through and brought healing to my mind, body, and soul. I praise Him and bless His name. I will forever praise the Lord and be grateful for all the many blessings and marvelous things He's done in my life. It is my hope that one day I will be able to join a mission and help spread the Word of the Lord to foreign nations. Traveling, helping others go through, and teaching about the wonders of our healer and wonderful Savior Jesus Christ truly would be a dream come true.

Traveling and sharing my story of how God brought me out continues to be a passion of mine. I feel the need to vent, if you will, so that non-believers will know that there is a God, a true and living God who is a healer and a protector. I am a witness to how God brings us through life's most difficult times, especially when nothing seems to be going our way. At all times we should have hope, faith, and trust in the Lord God Almighty, for He will bring us through. He will deliver, and I am a witness to this.

I did not understand many of the things that happened in my life. I often found myself on many occasions unsure of how I would make it to the very next day, week, or even this far. Sometimes, the winds blew so hard that all I could do was sit and cry. But when I found

Jesus and we both began to dig deep into my heart, mind, and spirit, there arose the will power I needed to get through life's challenges. No way did the hurt, pain, and suffering stop. It continued, and it still happens today. The challenges keep coming. But by faith and always looking up to the One that has brought me to this place I call T.H.R.O.U.G.H., I am victorious by trusting in God even the more.

> What shall we then say to these things? If God be for us, who can be against us? He that spared not His own Son, but delivered Him up for us all, how shall He not with Him also freely give us things? Who shall lay anything to the charge of God's elect? It is God that justifieth. Who is he that commandeth? It is Christ that died, yea rather, that is risen again, who is even at the right hand of God, who also maketh intercession for us.
>
> ROMANS 8:31-34

Although I could not understand the test most of the time, I praise God that He is greater than anything in this world. He is the solid rock. He is my life, my world, and my true friend. God has truly watched over me and kept me in the palm of His hand. Sadly, to many the love of God is not a story. Although written and historically recorded, many today still do not believe that Jesus sacrificed Himself for the sins of the world, rose from the grave, and now lives. The all too familiar saying, "Been there, done that," applies to me in this regard as well. I must admit that I did not always believe either. My life's journey has allowed me to arrive at the point where I now have greater faith, and each day I learn to look to God as I am now able to see His work in my life. Respect-fully, I know that God is who He says He is and is true in every regard.

God proved Himself to me in a great and magnificent way one evening as I was preparing to go to Bible study. It began to rain as it often had in the late evenings, but on this day to my amazement the clouds seemed so white — impressively bright white. The white clouds appeared to be much brighter than I had ever noticed. I often gazed at the clouds and watched its different formations. Striking-ly, there appeared a few dark clouds in the sky. As I stood at the door to watch the passing cars, a very large white cloud appeared directly over the entrance of my house. Unique as it was, undoubtedly something was taking place; as to what it was exactly, I was clueless. I knew that God was up to something and this was a good indicator of how His works and wonders were per-formed. As I continued to look at the cloud, I began to feel a cool sensation all over my body. This particular cloud seemed to be the only one in the bright blue sky that evening. Literally, it was hanging right in front of my house. Thus, as I looked into the bright white, unique form of the cloud, there was an urge to rejoice and praise the Lord. As I walked from room to room in my house, I began exclaiming, "Jesus, thank you, Lord! I praise you! I worship You! I love you, Lord! Thank You Lord!" There was something within and all I wanted to do was tell someone—anyone—of the beauty of the Lord.

During my chemotherapy treatments, I became more and more observant of the clouds, rain, and rivers. Unlike any other day, the pure whiteness and formation that appeared was like nothing I'd ever seen before. "What was God telling me now?" I asked myself. I knew it, I felt it, and I could not be persuaded that this was not God. What was I seeing? I could not take my eyes away. I was mesmerized and so genuinely excited that inwardly I began leaping for joy. As I continued to stare at the clouds, I began to feel the presence of God like never before. I became exceptionally moved by His presence. As I began to speak in the Spirit, I became refreshed and full of unusual excitement. At this point, I saw myself moving from place to place and from room to room. I just could not stop moving; I had to walk and talk, talk and walk. I was not in control of what I was doing; and moreover, it was refreshing, painless, and exhilarating. In those periods where I was sitting and watching others during my treatments, I often saw things which otherwise meant nothing or just simply appeared to be as they were. This epiphany was so amazing and awesome that I wanted to tell everyone of my experience. Just as my thoughts of wanting to share this vision became obvious, the clouds began moving, dissipating, and growing darker. Shortly thereafter, the rain came and then most of the white clouds disappeared.

My mind goes back to when I was a little girl growing up under spiritual and biblical teachings. My mother would point her finger toward me and say in a soft speaking voice that when the storm weather occurred, God was speaking. I was instructed to sit down and be quiet. I could be seen moving swiftly and hurriedly to a chair nearby. If my dad was home, I would run and sit on his lap, and amazingly, I would always find him with his arms open, knowing that I was on my way. My dad would tell me Bible stories until the weather passed over or I fell asleep. Mom would sit nearby on the sofa and smile as she watched me and my dad talk. Mom really did not say anything as Dad talked softly with me, given my mother's belief in total silence during stormy weather. My mother taught and was a firm believer in the fact that we should be respectful and submissive to God. As He spoke (through the weather), we were to sit and listen in total silence and obedience. Dad believed this as well but made an exception when I would run and sit on his lap during bad weather.

As I closely watched the shifting clouds, they suddenly changed position and color. Although the clouds began moving, I was still standing and walking through my house, rejoicing in the Spirit of the Lord. My emotional state had now been lifted to a place and stance like never before. My flesh felt different, my face was shining, and nothing seemed to be awry in my life. I was truly feeling God's covering upon me. I did not know then what His covering was preparing me for, but it would be essential in the months and days that lay ahead.

In the uniqueness of this, I began to think about what I was experiencing and who I could tell. I was hoping that my friend would arrive soon so I could share what I was experiencing and seeing. I wanted to tell someone! My excitement was overwhelming, and I thought that no one would believe what I saw unless they were witnessing it firsthand. As my emotions began to settle, I returned to the front door and began to stare once again at the brightness of the white clouds; and I was still taken aback. I don't think I will ever forget how God was preparing me for what would occur shortly thereafter.

(H)OLDING PLACE:
THE CELEBRATION

Holding place is a place of isolation and time of separation. As life presented me with many challenges—ups and downs—I found myself feeling lost and in a state of total separation from friends, family, and anyone that had a significant role in my life. I felt no connection to anyone. I felt there was nothing, nothing to be done but live each day as it came along. I had lost all hope and become so weak, yet I still wanted to live. I just did not seem to understand how to live and fulfil the promise or how to reach my destiny. Despite learning to become more disciplined and receiving a wealth of instruction, it just was not happening for me. I could not get to a place where I felt like I belonged. For so long I felt like no one cared, and whatever I said simply held no meaning to others. I'm sure you have been there and experienced this too!

The family and friends I was once surrounded by for most of my life seemed further and further away now. As the days and months passed, some of the same people who had helped nurture me had now received their calling from God to a new resting place. There was more pain, and it led to me feeling more and more isolated and lonely. I wondered frequently about what I was supposed to do. I questioned myself about what it was that I was supposed to be doing? In several conversations I've had with others, I have heard people admit that God allows certain things to happen to us for a reason. Yet, it occurred to me in my thoughts as to why things had been happening to me in the way that they had. Unbeknownst at that time, my ordination to develop this book was being established in me.

I was hurt and in much despair due to my past and all the crazy situations and circumstances that I had gone through. I was experiencing it so much that it almost felt normal. I was at a point where all my emotions seemed like glass that is shattered into a myriad of pieces. I had so much mixed emotions; I wanted to cry, but I ended up trying to pray. I cried time after time, and in my heart I knew deep down that God heard me. Unfortunately, I felt He just was not moving or responding fast enough. I was beginning to feel that a large part of me was beyond repair. I was so broken, that I was without hope. I wanted and needed someone to tell me what was wrong. I needed someone to tell me what I was not doing and what I had done wrong.

Have you ever felt like nothing was going right? Have you ever wondered if anyone really cared about you, what you were going through, what you had been through, or all that you had sacrificed in life? There was so much hurt that I began to journey down an avenue of isolation. I was not letting anyone in, and no one seemed to really want to be in my space. So, I just tuned out as much as I could. I did not see anything or anyone but my problems, conditions, and whatever each day brought. In my heart, I began to feel that this was it. Although I was still attending church and had limited socialization, those I did socialize with almost saluted my unhappiness. Shutting myself in and avoiding many of the local community residents felt like the right thing to do. I thought, *Who needs people to talk about you every day and act as though they had no problems and had everything going right for them?* No, I had no desire to be a part of their picture because I could not paint a bright picture for myself. So, the struggle continued. I was isolated and that made me feel so bent out of shape that I felt like I had no order to my life. But God was still working in me and through me. I just needed to throw the isolation trick of the devil back to where it was coming from.

After many months of being alone and not having many family members to reach out to, I eventually suffered an emotional breakdown. I didn't need to seek professional help nor did I make any attempt to hurt or harm myself. I just sat back and walked in each day just as it was. Television became an escape for me, and I immersed myself in a great deal of it. Many of the shows became reality for me. I found myself relating and identifying with many of the dramas on television as they became so real to me. The characters on these shows had marital problems, unpaid bills, and did not know where to find shelter from their storms. So, what was so different between my life and that of the characters on TV? What made the difference for me was that I had God on my side and my life was real, while television is just entertainment. I did not have to suffer anymore, but I could break free of this holding place, as television is designed to be informative and entertaining, offering many illusory shows and reality checks.

The shows that I frequently viewed just added to the picture that Satan had been pushing harder and deeper into my mind. "No hope," he said, "down and out you will remain—broken, never doing anything, and underachieving to the point of being an outright loser." I began to believe this for a long time. I watched people around me move to what seemed to be a prosperous life—new cars, houses, clothing, and whatever they desired. What I did not know as they were moving from one thing to the next was that they too experienced tests and hardships to get to where they were and maintain their state of accomplishment. I was in a holding place where everything that could hold me back or down, did. Satan used his tricks, and I was the victim, believing I was nothing. I fell into his trap because I was beaten in so many ways. Here is where the devil tricks us: using our minds and causing us to enter a place of isolation. The goal of Satan is obvious—he wants believers and people of faith to turn to him for help. As I watched many friends and family members strutting along what appeared to be a glamorous highway, jealousy arose within me. Now, clearly we know that's not a godly way of thinking. I was focusing on the material things and not on the love of God. Satan had me playing the major role in his movie. I was the star of the show. Through it all, God kept me safe in His arms, even when I thought I would not be able to see a clear light. God was there all the time. I had been so fooled by the devil and his games that I failed to reach out to the One who was keeping me day after day and situation after situation. God kept me; and I was neatly tucked in His arms of protection, prepared to enter a new day and season for Kingdom building.

Going through made all the difference now because it gave me the strength, vision, and ability to rise, even in spite of what the devil's plan was. The adversary's plan was to destroy me, and he wanted me to be the laughingstock of the town. Who did I think I was to rise above his mess? God was there all the time; but because I could not see Him, simply put, I did not believe it. Isolation felt right and like a safe place, but this was only the adversary playing tricks on me. Despite the devil's tactics, my strength was being renewed, and I would soon reach a point of renewal in my mind, body, and spirit. I would arrive at a new depot in which isolation would no longer have control, and my entire being—my womanhood, motherhood, Christian walk and talk—would be reconstructed. I had to reach out and take control of my destiny and let God do what He was waiting to do. God wanted to revive me. I was already molded from birth, but now God wanted to shape and mold me into a new creature for His use.

For we are his workmanship, created in Christ Jesus
unto good works, which God hath before ordained that
we should walk in them.

EPHESIANS 2:10 (KJV)

There is hope, and there is a wonderful life in living
for Jesus Christ. Revived, restored, and reconstructed—
living all for the glory of the Lord has made the difference for me. I was equipped from birth by God, and there
will be no holding me back from what God has chosen
for me. I was redeemed through the finished work of
Christ. My place of T.H.R.O.U.G.H. was just my destiny
calling me to follow the Lord. I was called to love Him
even the more because He lives and because His love was
neatly unfolding within me.

As I pondered and thought about Peter in the middle
of the ocean—wind howling, darkness, and high tides
rolling as the water filled their boat—he and the disciples
were safe, even though their circumstance would have
said otherwise. Jesus was amid the storm, and as in my
life, Jesus did not let any hurt or harm come upon them.
Imagine with me for a moment, Peter gazing at the rag-
ing sea. Can you picture what his thoughts, fears, and
panic must have been like?

Thinking about Peter's quandary and the uneasiness
he must have felt causes me to reflect on the days that I

traveled to the doctor's office at the cancer treatment center. I tried very hard to press and pray my way through the treatments in the midst of my discomfort and apprehension. I often wondered about what God was trying to tell me and what He wanted me to see throughout the whole ordeal. Truly, it is a blessing to have a relationship with God. It is pure joy when we know Him as our Redeemer who lived, suffered, bled, and died for all of our sins at Calvary. My love for God is not just contingent upon Him bringing me through many storms, but it is for the mere, simple fact that I just love Him for whom He is. For as long as I live I will praise, trust, worship, and exalt Him forever. John 15:1-2 affirms: "I am the true vine, and my Father is the husbandman. Every branch in me that beareth not fruit He taketh away: and every branch that beareth fruit, He purgeth it, that it may bring forth more fruit." It is when we make a conscious effort to always abide in Him, that He reveals more of Himself to and through us.

As the days began to pass, day after day, I began to struggle with doubt and fear, as help from the friends, resources, and people I knew seemed to be scarce and not present at all in some instances. It was when I opened my mouth and my mind that I began to release the hurt. God let me know that He was still standing with me every step of the way—through the storm, the wind, and now the rain that poured and kept pouring in the midst of my fear, hurt, pain, and doubt.

Reflecting on the story of Peter, we see clearly a man that knew God as he no longer walked in himself but yielded to the Spirit of God and His power to save him from destruction. It was in the midst of his turmoil and trauma that Peter began to realize who was with him. Jesus wanted Peter to believe in Him and not doubt. Just as my experience occurred, I had arrived, and I needed to get T.H.R.O.U.G.H. Destiny awaited and had been calling me all the time. I was hearing what I wanted to hear, and I was not allowing God's voice or message to penetrate my mind. There was so much confusion, heartache, pain, and constant turmoil in my life. At times, nothing seemed to matter. But here I was now, standing amid a real life-threatening storm and treading the waves of the sea. I was traveling—traveling toward my destiny. I was born again. I was set free from bondage and the hurtful feelings that emanated from my past. I died mentally from the stress and physical pain that always seemed to continually occur. Miraculously and wondrously, I made it to a temporary holding place of peace and clearer thinking. God had promised me that I would see brighter days and He would walk beside me as I continued my journey.

Walking and living for Christ often entails pain, sorrow, and heartaches; but there is victory that always follows. After all, the adversary doesn't want us to live happily, be totally committed, and be in love with the Lord God Almighty. But God did give His promise that victory at the end of our trial, test, and suffering would be ours if we would only believe.

> No temptation has overtaken you except what is common to mankind. And God is faithful; he will not let you be tempted beyond what you can bear. But when you are tempted, he will also provide a way out so that you can endure it.
>
> 1 CORINTHIANS 10:13 (NIV)

So why not give Christ our all? Accept Him as King of kings, Lord of lords, and the ever-loving Savior. Give Him your all because He suffered, was laughed at, beaten, and crucified for you. Christ did it all because He loved us all. I will ever be thankful that God has taken me through. It is pure love, joy, and happiness in knowing that God will always take us through the tough times, and He is more than just a way-maker or provider. He is a father as well. Knowing Him as a Father who cares for and loves His children is an awesome experience. I began to realize that there are times in our life when we must suffer and when we must go through

150

what seems impossible. Moreover, it is Jesus, our keeper, who gives us the necessary strength to continue living according to His will. I had to surrender my all to my heavenly Father, even if it would cost the life of a loved one or even mine. Obedience was and is essential to getting through. Jesus was obedient to His Father when He went to Calvary. So why then do we fight—mentally, physically, and spiritually—to get T.H.R.O.U.G.H? Jesus' path for me to T.H.R.O.U.G.H was the route that I call Grace Highway. Now, here I am. I stand tall and empowered with hope; and I live by the Word of God. I have faith, and I believe in the Father, Jesus' burial and resurrection, and that He will return one day.

Now, just because I had survived deaths in the family, rejection, and a terminal illness doesn't mean that the worst was over and it was all good after that. It is amazing that before I could get to the end of this chapter of my life, my faith was tested again; and I was truly in a storm. I found myself needing more will power, and I had to find the answer to how I could rise above the circumstance and situation.

IN THE HEAT OF THE NIGHT

It was shortly after midnight one night—nothing but darkness, and street lights nowhere in sight in the rural area that I live in. Even the stars were hardly visible, and everything seemed to be still, still as though there was no life in the environment. I could not feel or sense the danger that lingered near; but it was close, creeping in, and lurked just around the corner. On this particular evening, my son had just gotten home, and we began to shut down for the night. Within minutes there came a loud bang at the front door. It wasn't two or three bangs but one earth-shattering knock. My son, as he heard the loud bang, departed from his bedroom and made his way into the living room, only to be met by a gang of gunmen. There was no time to prepare or arm ourselves with anything after the gunmen barged through the front door. From my bedroom I could see a gun being wielded in the living room. As I arose out of my bed and began to enter the living room, I did not know what I would do, I just knew I had to get out of bed and move slowly into the living room. As I entered the living room, the gunmen demanded that I sit down on the couch. As my heart pounded in distress, the only thing my eyes could see was the gun being pointed at me and my son. My heart jumped and danced around like it wasn't even restricted by the confines of my body. It was almost as though I could not feel anything. I obliged with one of the gunman's command to sit on the couch, but my son advised them that I had difficulty sitting down on a low seat because of a knee injury that I had sustained previously. Surprisingly, the gunmen said, "I know." I sat there quietly, but internally I was heavily distressed. It was almost as if my heart was shedding tears, and these tears were imminently about to appear on my face. On the inside I was seeking God for help. I began to panic as one of the intruders made demands on my son, who happens to be handicapped. I stared and looked at my child. I couldn't help but be unnerved at the sight of my oldest son being in harm's way. Fear highlighted his face as the intruder commanded him, and it was very difficult to watch. What was I to do? How could I help him? I could not use the phone since it wasn't nearby, and I could not reach the panic button on the wall-mounted alarm system's control panel. Neither could I get to the gun that we kept hidden in the house. I could not cry out loud or say anything for that matter. As I stared through the now open front door that had just been kicked in by the gunmen, I looked into the darkness. There was pure darkness now, and not even a star could be seen in the sky. All I saw was the darkness that lingered and the treetops in the yard. No cars or trucks were moving; nothing passed by on the street. I felt empty emotionally. I had reached a point where I could not even shout, "Jesus," but all I could do was sit and watch what was happening to my son. All I could do was wonder where our help would come from.

Eventually, the gunmen exited my home, leaving the front door wide open. I suggested to my son that we sit still until we knew that they were gone for sure. Momentarily, I saw what seemed like a flash in the bushes. As we waited, it was hard to talk, but I knew it was truly a time to trust God more than ever. Somehow, I just knew that sitting still would make the difference. Sitting still, I could and did allow God to have control of the situation. I did not have to shout, yell, or cry. My son and I just had to let God work a miracle. I sat motionless and began to recite Psalm 23 silently in my mind.

> The LORD is my shepherd; I shall not want. He maketh me to lie down in green pastures: He leadeth me beside the still waters. He restoreth my soul: He leadeth me in the paths of righteousness for His name's sake. Yea, though I walk through the valley of the shadow of death, I will fear no evil: for thou art with me; thy rod and thy staff they comfort me. Thou preparest a table before me in the presence of mine enemies: thou anointest my head with oil; my cup runneth over. Surely goodness and mercy shall follow me all the days of my life: and I will dwell in the house of the LORD forever.
>
> PSALM 23

Minutes later, we were able to get our phones and call for help, which arrived shortly thereafter. Although we were distressed emotionally, thank God we were not harmed in any physical sense. Without a doubt I knew in my spirit and mind that we had something to praise God for like never before. Praising God became significantly more important as I watched the terror on my son's face. As the 911 call went out and we sat waiting for help to arrive, God gave us another chance to live and a chance to be His servants.

God wants us to give Him glory and not render it to worldly things. He wants His praise, He wants us to love Him, and He deserves all that we can give Him. Since He gave us His Son, we owe everything to Him. The lesson learned from this predicament was that God still reigns over your life even when facing a tragedy. After this incident, I began to think about many things. My emotional state had been somewhat paralyzed, but even in that condition God revealed many things to me. To be exact, I was reminded about Peter and the disciples and how they too weathered the dark, high tide and wind blowing at sea. I can only imagine the fear and the coldness of the rising waves, but standing there in the midst of the storm, high winds, and tides was Jesus. Jesus my Savior was Jesus at sea—reaching, watching, and reigning in His entire splendor, as Peter—much like me—came to the realization that it was Jesus who was right there all the time and had never left his presence. Whatever storm you find yourself going through, always know that Jesus is there with you.

> Now faith is being sure of what we hope for, being convinced of what we do not see.
>
> HEBREWS 11:1 (NET)

After the invasion had ended, I thanked God and reminded my son that it was time to pray and glorify God. I encouraged him to attend church for spiritual growth as I had learned to do over the years. Church and Bible study were of high regard to me. It was my hope that this incident would propel my son to convert to Christ, change his thoughts and lifestyle, and seek the Lord; for the hand of the Lord was truly present with us. God's loving arms shielded and protected us from what very well could have been the end of life on earth for the both of us, but we are blessed to still have life today.

Amazing grace was on our side, and nothing will ever compare to the saving grace of the Lord God Almighty. After the invasion, I then received revelation as to what God was telling me when I experienced the appearance of those bright white clouds over my house on that night I was preparing for Bible study. During the darkest of nights, God saw our need and met the need through His protection; He covered us from the danger that was upon us. Standing by our side was Almighty God—El-Shaddai—who was working behind the scenes in my life and my son's. In fact, this situation had a forceful impact on some friends and relatives. It is amazing how fast news spreads throughout the community when things go wrong! Yet, none of our neighbors came immediately after seeing all the police cars parked in our yard to see if they could offer any help. As daylight dawned on the horizon, only those whom my son and I had called actually came to help out. After the incident it was also startling to see people's reaction toward us when we would cross paths in public. They looked at us as if we were ghosts and with amazed faces would quietly say, "I heard what happened." There was no doubt in my mind that the community was singing the news about what had happened, singing like the birds I heard chirping outside my house every morning. As time passed on, a few friends from neighboring communities reached out with sincere empathy, and some family members who had helped me in the past also lent their support and aid.

God manifested Himself as Jehovah-Shammah (the Lord is present) and was the only friend I needed. Who then is a better friend? Believe me, there is none like Him. Jesus met our needs, and although I could not see Him in the physical sense, He was there from the very first kick on the door up until the intruders' exit. What a mighty God we serve! Hallelujah!

As help arrived and law enforcement investigated the scene, I had a sense of emptiness stirring within me. I had to find a place to get through this ordeal. It was late at night, and I did not want to wake anyone up. My son urged me to call someone in order to calm my nerves and receive some solace. He wanted me to speak to someone, but I was more concerned about his welfare since the intruders had left the scene in fury and rage after they were unable to procure the item that they thought my son had.

As the days and months passed, we were clearly able to see the calling of God and His desire upon our lives. I know there is much work to be done, and there are people like those of you reading my story that need help getting T.H.R.O.U.G.H. I encourage you to hold on to God, seek Him with all that is within you, praise Him for all the things He's done, and thank Him in advance for what He's still working out for you and your family. Somewhere, I'm sure there is someone that may be hurting from and even crying about similar experiences. You may be perturbed and frustrated; but what I hope to share and inspire in others is that no matter what your situation or circumstance may be, you're never alone. It's just a matter of trusting God and letting Him work things out. Life will present things in such a way that may make you feel hopeless, be doubtful, and experience despair but do not by any means give up. Never give in to the doubt, fear, and hopelessness. Trust God even the more. Faith, hope, God's love, and having a relationship with the Lord will guide you through life's journey. My situations and the many circumstances could have been worse; but God, our heavenly Father, knew my heart. I trust Him with one hundred percent of my being, today and forever. God has paved the way for our very existence. Isaiah 49:15-16 states: "Can a mother forget the baby at her breast and have no compassion on the child she has borne? Though she may forget, I will not forget you! See, I have engraved you on the palms of my hands; your walls are ever before me" (NIV).

Thinking back to my relationship with my mother, she was preparing me for the days ahead, and in many instances I did not want to hear what she had to say. Sometimes I even attempted to walk away, but I later regretted doing so. Thanks be to God for a praying mother, who never gave up on me or my sons. God allowed me for such a wonderful season to find the true mother-daughter relationship. So here I am now, still learning and hoping to help my children, their children, and people across the nation to know the meaning of true love—love like no other which is the love of God that makes life worthwhile despite what we may go through. I hope and pray that my sons and the sons of others will in time kneel down, humble themselves, and pray.

> if my people who are called by my name humble themselves, and pray and seek my face, and turn from their wicked ways, then I will hear from heaven and will forgive their sin and heal their land. Now, my eyes will be open and my ears attentive to the prayer that is made in this place. For now, I have chosen and consecrated this house that my name may be there forever. My eyes and my heart will be there for all time. And as for you, if you will walk before me as David your father walked, doing according to all that I have commanded you and keeping my statutes and my rules, then I will establish your royal throne, as I covenanted with David your father, saying, 'You shall not lack a man to rule Israel.'
>
> 2 CHRONICLES 7:14-18 (ESV)

Now, I am not saying that my son doesn't pray or seek the Lord. He is simply doing things his way until God changes him in His own way! I realize and know that Jehovah-Shammah, our Creator, knows his heart, thoughts, and ways. Yet, as each day passes and when the nights seem longer and darker at times, God is still working on and watching over us. He's here and will forever be!

Much like the apostle Peter began sinking when he was walking on the water, I too had gotten caught up in my surroundings and my feelings. Instead of always walking by faith, I will admit that during some of my dilemmas I often paid more attention to what I could detect with my physical senses and fell victim to my emotions. It is my prayer that God will continue to use me as a vessel to empower my son and many other mothers and their children with God's love as they journey T.H.R.O.U.G.H. My desire is to tell my story from nation to nation and country to country because God has brought me thus far, and I am a true witness that no matter what life presents, God will always bring you through. Just stand in faith, hope, and love and wait on God. Patiently wait, even when it's difficult, and He will answer.

As a mother who cares, I pray that my life and my love for God will display hope and learning to live each day falling in continual love with the Lord God Almighty. Our children and families are gifts from God, not some science project or experiment but God's handiwork and creation. Furthermore, it is written that genuine love—unconditionally loving Him and one another as Christ loves us—is a must if we are to live a holy life.

Imitate God, therefore, in everything you do, because you are His dear children. Live a life filled with love, following the example of Christ. He loved us and offered Himself as a sacrifice for us, a pleasing aroma to God.

EPHESIANS 5:1-2 (NLT)

God created man in His own image, and His image is holy and sinless. As children of the heavenly Father, we have been instructed to be like Him from the beginning of time throughout all eternity! Additionally, we are to be holy in all of our ways, reflecting whom we are fashioned in the image of.

(R)EVIVAL: THE CRY OF RENEWAL, RECOVERY, RESTORATION, AND RECONSTRUCTION

As my life presented many challenges—many of them in different ways—I discovered a place of renewal in my life. I found a pool of cleansing, healing, and deliverance. I was healed from my past faults and from all the past emotions of bitterness and hatred that had plagued me for so long. I was no longer in a place where nothing seemed to matter. Everything matters now; and I have a better sense of thinking and hope for change. I relocated and took ownership of the hope that was lost. I no longer accepted the hurt and disappointments that came my way. I knew the Lord was answering my prayers, and He truly heard my heart's cry as I lay awake throughout the dark and lonely midnight hours that never seemed to end. Now, the past was just that—the past. Game over. The time arrived for me to recover and renew my thinking. It was reconstruction time, and the walls of destruction had to come down. I refused to let the walls fall upon or destroy me as I tore them down, bit by bit, piece by piece, and cell by cell. The wall and path of destruction were gone, and God's Word reaffirmed that it was.

> According as His divine power hath given unto us all things that pertain unto life and godliness, through the knowledge of Him that hath called us to glory and virtue: Whereby are given unto us exceeding great and precious promises: that by these ye might be partakers of the divine nature, having escaped the corruption that is in the world through lust. And beside this, giving all diligence, add to your faith virtue; and to virtue knowledge; And to knowledge temperance; and to temperance patience; and to patience godliness; And to godliness brotherly kindness; and to brotherly kindness charity. For if these things be in you, and abound, they make you that ye shall neither be barren nor unfruitful in the knowledge of our Lord Jesus Christ. But he that lacketh these things is blind, and cannot see afar off, and hath forgotten that he was purged from his old sins. Wherefore the rather, brethren, give dili-

gence to make your calling and election sure: for if ye do these things, ye shall never fall.

2 PETER 1:3-10

I was designed to be uniquely created in the image of Christ. After enduring so many challenging circumstances, the experience and pressure of feeling like an absolute failure developed into feelings of being disliked. I had undergone a great deal of mental and physical abuse and learned to tolerate it. But thank God for His healing and deliverance. I found what was and remains to be the greatest revelation: acceptance of Jesus as my Savior. I reached a place of knowing that there's safety in the arms of the Lord. I no longer had to worry about being accepted by friends or family. I had Jesus on my side and in my heart. Jesus accepted me the way I was and for whom I have become today.

Surely, I still wear many of the scars from my past. However, they merely remain in my thoughts as a reminder of what I have gone through and how God took me through the test. God renewed within me a peace that I never imagined I could have. God placed in my mind, body, and soul the kind of peace that makes everything worthwhile at the end of the day. My past was a time of preparation; and I was being prepared for a new walk and journey—my destiny! Did Satan leave me alone? Oh no, he still attacks me to this very day, but now I have greater will power. I can rise as I continue to lean and depend on the One who has all the power and gives me strength to exist.

There is no more procrastinating, as this was a thing long gone, and it was time to get things moving. It is celebration time—celebration time for my journey as I begin to walk and talk about the goodness of Jesus and all He has brought me through. I am now at the point which I hear the questions: Who are you talking to? Where are you walking to? With whom are you walking? I am walking in faith, hope, and God's love—nothing less. More determined to live and not die, I had to continue this battle on my journey to get T.H.R.O.U.G.H.

And we know that the Son of God is come, and hath given us an understanding, that we may know him that is true, and we are in him that is true, even in his Son Jesus Christ. This is the true God, and eternal life.

1 JOHN 5:20

When I strayed and fell away from the will of God, He still kept me in His will. I traveled through the valley of darkness, and I walked in the shadow of death. But the Lord kept me and taught me not to fear any evil; for God, my Father, was and remains with me day after day. My Father is always with me. He is the rod and staff that guides and directs me; yet, He provides comfort when I am weary and consoles me when I feel despair. When my enemies surround me, my God has already prepared a table before me in their presence. I'm truly anointed, restored, and set free in Jesus. My head, my thoughts, and my being have been refreshed with the sweet oil of a new life. My cup overflows with joy, happiness, peace, long-suffering, and meekness.

> But the fruit of the Spirit is love, joy, peace, long-suffering, gentleness, goodness, faith. Meekness, temperance: against such there is no law. And they that are Christ's have crucified the flesh with the affections and lusts. If we live in the Spirit, let us also walk in the Spirit.
>
> GALATIANS 5:22-25

Surely, His goodness and mercy shall follow me all the days of my life. Wherein, I shall dwell in the house and in the presence of the Lord forever and ever.

> I lift up my eyes toward the mountains from where will my help come? My help is from the Lord, maker of heaven and earth. He will never let your foot slip, nor will your guardian become drowsy. Look! The one who is guarding Israel never sleeps and does not take naps. The Lord is your guardian; the Lord is your shade at your right side. The sun will not ravage you

by day, nor the moon by night. The Lord will guard you from all evil, preserving your life. The Lord will guard your goings and comings, from this time on and forever.

PSALM 121 (ISV)

Jesus is such a wonderful friend and teacher. He's my comforter and my everything. He's my life. Jesus is the light that continually guides me from the darkness and darkest places. It is the love of my Father that shines ever so bright within me. I can see now. Hallelujah! I've found in Jesus all that I ever longed for. I found love, peace, and joy. I'm no longer blinded by the enemy and his tricks. When the enemy strikes, I call on Jesus. I have come to a place where I am leaning on the arms of Jesus.

A critical lesson that I have learned is that when the attacks come, I should call on the greatest name—Jesus. I can't thank God enough for saving me from destruction and bringing me to this point and place in time of reconstruction. I thank God for allowing me to go through the turbulence and bringing me to a place where everything I go through only fortifies my new walk by edifying and allowing me to teach and instruct others who desire to grow in the Lord. Had I stayed the course and continued on the path that I was journeying on, my life literally would have ended. I suffered so much to the point that the pathway seemed narrower and narrower. But God was and is so much bigger. God allowed my valley to grow dark and dreary for a reason, although I didn't know why nor did I understand the many mysteries of my life. Life for me would have continued to exist according to the desires and pleasures of the world if it had not been for God's love and will. Had I not chosen the Lord as my keeper and lover of my soul, I would have remained lost and would still be tossed around. Thankfully, I found a Savior who really cares and opened my heart to His love. Our Father in heaven is so awesome. He gives us all we ask for when we believe and live according to His commandments.

> Believe me that I am in the Father, and the Father in me: or else believe me for the very works' sake. Verily, verily, I say unto you, He that believeth on me, the works that I do shall he do also; and greater works than these shall he do; because I go unto my Father. And whatsoever ye shall ask in my name, that will I do, that the Father may be glorified in the Son. If ye shall ask any thing in my name, I will do it. If ye love me, keep my commandments.
>
> JOHN 14:11-15

Our loving Father provides His love and only asks that we keep His commandments. Jesus, even in His infinite wisdom and determination to save souls, still grew weary at Calvary. Even though His life on earth was fading fast, He carried the sins of mankind to the cross despite the fact that He was sinless. With His life, He paid the highest price ever for mankind. Jesus was faced with disappointment. He felt physical and mental pain— mentally the pain of being betrayed, feeling abandoned, and no longer hearing from the Father, the person who sent Him. Jesus experienced being tired; and He faced temptation and apprehension too.

> Therefore he had to be made like his brothers in every respect, so that he might become a merciful and faithful high priest in the service of God, to make propitiation for the sins of the people.
>
> HEBREWS 2:17 (ESV)

> And saith unto them, My soul is exceeding sorrowful unto death: tarry ye here, and watch. And he went forward a little, and fell on the ground, and prayed that, if it were possible, the hour might pass from him. And he said, Abba, Father, all things are possible unto thee; take away this cup from me: nevertheless not what I will, but what thou wilt.
>
> MARK 14:34-36

As my life grew and my weariness increased, I too learned to lean on the only One that could save me from destruction. Jesus cried out to His Father, who sent Him to save a dying world; and I too had to learn to cry out to the Father, my sustainer, in preparation for what was to come.

CANNOT BE DENIED

Today, I am victorious, but on the other hand, there are many today that won't acknowledge Christ or call His wonderful name. As for me, the name of Jesus has given me hope for each day and the strength to sustain myself day after day. I remember as a child when I would see the stores decorated with bright lights and moving fixtures during Christmas time. What stood out to me was that "Christmas" was spelled X-MAS! After having reached a certain level of maturity, I began to wonder, *Wow, how could people make and take such efforts to eliminate the name of Christ from such a celebration of life?* Although He was wounded, carried the cross on His back, bled, and died for the salvation of all mankind, many people today still prefer to use X-MAS. Glory to the King! Jesus is our protector; and He is higher than any mountain and higher than the storms of life. I am truly thankful to God for every step, every mountain, and every breath I take.

I have become ever so grateful for every victory I have achieved and for knowing that I am victorious in all things because of my Savior. As I climb and reach higher heights in life's journey, I have found and learned the true assurance I have in my heavenly Father, the assurance that guides me T.H.R.O.U.G.H. As I now reflect over my life, where I have been, and where I am now, it genuinely amazes me how God has guided and protected me when I was so ignorant of His calling on my life. The inspiration of Scripture provides us with much hope and assurance.

> Little children, you belong to God and have overcome them, because the one who is in you is greater than the one who is in the world. These people belong to the world. That is why they speak from the world's perspective, and the world listens to them. We belong to God. The person who knows God listens to us. Whoever does not belong to God does not listen to us. This is how we know the Spirit of truth and the spirit of deceit.
>
> 1 JOHN 4:4-6 (ISV)

God has brought me to a place of renewal, restoration, and reconstruction. There's no turning back to the "stinking thinking" or desires of the world. My desire is to serve the Lord wholeheartedly. I want and am aiming to be a passionate steward for Christ. With all that I am and all that He desires of me, it is imperative for me to become a true servant, leader, follower, witness for

Christ, and worthy daughter of God. I have truly been renewed in my thoughts and my actions. Although I am often misunderstood and sometimes experience feelings of being unappreciated, I see clearly where I have come from and what I stand for. I truly am renewed. Praise the Lord for His goodness. I thank God for saving me and giving me a heart to love and a heart to live and worship truthfully in the Spirit and newness of Christ.

> Make me to hear joy and gladness; that the bones which thou hast broken may rejoice. Hide thy face from my sins, and blot out all mine iniquities. Create in me a clean heart, O God; and renew a right spirit within me. Cast me not away from your presence; and take not thy Holy Spirit from me. Restore unto me the joy of thy salvation; and uphold me with thy free spirit.
>
> PSALM 51:8-10

God did it; He was working faithfully in me, my attitude, my speech, and everything that I am. I just could not see it, nor was I willing to accept or consent to walk in the path ordained for myself. Thank God, for He gave me a second chance to discover and work toward His desires and will for my life. Hallelujah! I praise God for all that He has put into renewing me. I have walked through the valley, and been through many storms and tests. Nonetheless, God did not let me die, but He brought me through the hardest part of growth and spiritual maturity. God's ultimate plan and reconstruction of my existence is so that He would be pleased with whom I am. God has not ignored my failures, my disbelief, or the occasional unwillingness to serve Him. It's not about what the world said I would be or the composition of my DNA. God's divine and ultimate reconstruction of my life is all that matters. Here, now I stand on Christ—my everything, my life, my purpose, and whatever I desire in Him.

BEHOLD THE LOVE OF GOD

The story of Nehemiah (a layman and butler to the Persian emperor Artaxerxes) testifies of one's struggles and triumph. Nehemiah means "God Comforts" or "Comforted of Yah." Nehemiah was entrusted with a prominent position of serving during the era of one of the most powerful rulers and assigned the task of cupbearer to the king. Additionally, as the cupbearer he possessed the responsibility of tasting the wine of the king to ensure that it had not been poisoned. The role of cupbearer was an office of great responsibility, power, and honor in the Persian Empire. Not only was the cupbearer a personal servant but also a trusted confidant and advisor. Nehemiah gained the trust and confidence of the king, which was significant to his being appointed to rule as governor in Jerusalem. What characteristics do you hold that gives someone in a prominent position the confidence to trust in you? Is it your patience, charm, or behavior? For me, it's my love for God and my daily walk—the way I live, talk, and worship unconditionally.

One day, Nehemiah received upsetting information in regard to the state of affairs of the Jewish people. Think about your reaction when you receive disturbing news regarding a friend, family member, or the world news viewed on television or heard over the radio waves. Nehemiah was overwhelmingly upset by the news, but he sought help from the one, true source which was strong enough to bring him, you, and me to victory. I am sure that Nehemiah and many of us have learned that fasting, praying, and listening with an open mind and heart allows God to intervene and teach us to have compassion for others as we travel through life. Thus, it is essential to our existence and relationship with the Lord that we treat our friends, family, loved ones, and everyone with love just as Jesus loves us. It is the will of God that we live in harmony with everyone, even our enemies.

> But to you who are listening I say: Love your enemies, do good to those who hate you, bless those who curse you, pray for those who mistreat you. If someone slaps you on one cheek, turn to them the other also. If someone takes your coat, do not withhold your shirt from them. Give to everyone who asks you, and if anyone

takes what belongs to you, do not demand it back. Do to others as you would have them do to you.

LUKE 6:27-31 (NIV)

Nehemiah accepted and received permission to leave Persia and return to Jerusalem to take on the task of rebuilding the walls of Jerusalem. Nehemiah ventured out for this feat with a determined heart and mind to do the will of God and help his people. Kindheartedly, Nehemiah chose to seek God, appealing to God for understanding and wisdom as he prepared for the task that lay ahead. Nehemiah knew that God was a God of truth and would guide him, believing that God would grant him the strength and necessary courage to fulfill the immense commission.

> When I heard these words I sat down and wept, and mourned for days; and I continued fasting and praying before the God of heaven.
>
> NEHEMIAH 1:4 (RSV)

My calling and purpose is to teach and inspire others to walk in and aspire to live in God's love by helping them to pray and believe in the power granted to tear down the strongholds hindering them from reaching their destiny. My calling is not an easy task, much like any task that is ordained by God. Nevertheless, our God-given assignment is His will even though the adversary stirs quickly and will try to distract us whenever we're walking and living according to the will and instructions of the Father.

Life will take us to a point where giants seem so tall and almost unmovable. Certainly, I can attest to the fact of having had many giants in my path, and I'm sure you will agree that you've had many as well. Circumstances that I faced were the giants in my life that just would not seem to fade away no matter what I did. However, when I learned to rest in the love of God, the things that appeared to be giants were truly so much smaller than I envisioned. After having frequently searched within myself, now I have learned to boldly seek God for guidance, wisdom, and understanding of my calling as my charge becomes clearer and clearer each day. Do you and are you seeking the Lord when faced with oppression, life challenges, and the fiery darts of Satan? I have arrived at a place and time in my life where prayer has become an essential role for my daily living. I can't go without it; and amid a busy day or night, prayer has become a part of my deepest thoughts. I have found myself waking in the middle of the night, only to fall asleep praying and praising God.

At the stage where I am now, prayer is no longer a forced effort, nor do I do it out of obligation as some religious act that is required of us daily. It became and has become a part of me because I believe in what prayer will do; and I can attest to the fact that prayer works. Look at me; it has been through the power of my prayers and even those of my parents and guardians that I am here today. I believe prayer comes from an individual's heart and is representative of one's relationship with the Lord. I can pray for you, you can pray for me, we can pray for each other, but what matters is the sincerity of our prayers and our relationship with God. I know that God hears and answers my prayers. Were it not for Him hearing and answering the prayers from my crying heart, I would have fallen—fallen far from my destiny. I truly desire a stronger relationship—like no other—with God. Therefore, daily devotion and prayer is the norm for me now, and I don't just pray for myself either. I pray for others who are going through things and learning to walk in hope, faith, and God's love.

> No temptation has overtaken you that is not common to man. God is faithful, and He will not let you be tempted beyond your ability, but with the temptation He will also provide the way of escape, that you may be able to endure it.
>
> 1 CORINTHIANS 10:13 (ESV)

I thank God for His many blessings and for bringing me T.H.R.O.U.G.H. Like Nehemiah who was faced with a struggle, I began to trust God to fight my battles and guide me through. Although battles, trials, and temptations will come and go time after time, having the love of God will wipe away all the fears, tears, heartaches, pain, and suffering. Jesus died, but He rose again in three days—victorious over death after sacrificing Himself for us. Because He saves us and bestows blessings upon us, we must celebrate Him on a daily basis by loving Him and praising Him. My breakthrough has led to security, protection, and greater hope and trust in the Lord God my Shepherd.

> O Lord, let thy ear be attentive to the prayer of thy servant, and to the prayer of thy servants who delight to fear thy name; and give success to thy servant today.
>
> NEHEMIAH 1:11 (RSV)

Unselfishly, Nehemiah sought the Lord's help not just for himself; but he beseeched Jehovah-Jireh's divine intervention for others' lives as well. It is always a blessing when we can pray for others in addition to ourselves, especially when we are mistreated by others. It is in our best interest to pray for them because God will bring us T.H.R.O.U.G.H. when we do so. Honestly, I now confess to praying when I've been treated wrongly and unfairly.

It was Nehemiah's request that God would reposition the heart of King Ahasuerus. I also desire that God would reposition the hearts of many friends and family members that have mistreated me, not just in my past but also in my present state of renewal, recovery, restoration, and reconstruction.

Gifts of love granted by our heavenly Father initiated my season of restoration and revival. As a result, I am essentially reconstructed to who I was designed to be for Kingdom building; and the walls which have been reconstructed restored order in life. Peace is ours, joy is ours, and promising futures all belong to us because of the love of the Lord and His promises. This was my gift from the day I was born, but I just had to discover and use it like never before.

Nehemiah had a plan. What's your plan? Will you follow Jesus and let Him be your guide? Will you attempt over and over to reconstruct your thoughts and actions on your own, building walls that will fall? Nehemiah had a clear understanding of what he needed to do. He saw the vision, he understood the plan, and he was committed to reconstructing the wall. Are you committed to seeking the Lord and allowing Him in your heart to reconstruct the wall that will stand for life?

Nehemiah, empowered by God, duly established assignments to each person who was willing to work on building the wall. This reminds me of the way a pastor, supervisor, teacher, or anyone in authority might ask us to take on a job. Sometimes we may not be willing, and other times we *are* willing; but we become anxious for various reasons. As a team player, role model, or leader, we have a responsibility to each other to fulfil our tasks. Thus, when one falls out of line, our role must include picking up the pieces and helping others get through. Have you chosen anyone to help build your wall, your faith, or your walk in life according to the will and instructions of our heavenly Father? The wall that Nehemiah was commissioned to build had several gates. The order of the gates as stated in the book of Nehemiah has symbolic significance. Taking a didactic look at the construction sequence of these gates reveals that the order in which they were built represents, and in a way, parallels the process of human salvation—our order, pattern of growth, and maturity in the things of God.

The twelve gates Nehemiah endeavored to rebuild in Jerusalem are in order as follows: The Sheep Gate, Fish Gate, Old Gate, Valley Gate, Dung Gate, Fountain Gate, Water Gate, Horse Gate, East Gate, and Miphkad (Inspection) Gate. Meaningfully, the twelve gates symbolically relate to our life experiences in reaching the place called T.H.R.O.U.G.H. Traveling through these gates is necessary for each one of us.

SHEEP GATE

Restoration and reconstruction of the gates began with the Sheep Gate. The Sheep Gate—gate of sacrifice—was where the sheep were brought into Jerusalem to be sacrificed. The Sheep Gate represents fulfillment, and it represents God in every sense, including His love and hope that we would live in unity and lead others to Him. Symbolically, the Sheep Gate also announces the Lamb of God, Jesus Christ, who would come to take the sins of the world upon Himself.

> The next day John saw Jesus coming toward him and said, "Look! The Lamb of God who takes away the sin of the world! He is the one I was talking about when I said, 'A man is coming after me who is far greater than I am, for he existed long before me.' I did not recognize him as the Messiah, but I have been baptizing with water so that he might be revealed to Israel." Then John testified, "I saw the Holy Spirit descending like a dove from heaven and resting upon him. I didn't know he was the one, but when God sent me to baptize with water, he told me, 'The one on whom you see the Spirit descend and rest is the one who will baptize with the

Holy Spirit.' I saw this happen to Jesus, so I testify that he is the Chosen One of God.

JOHN 1: 29-34 (NLT)

The Sheep Gate denotes forgiveness of sins for the sake of Jesus' redemption in His blood. This gate asserts the forgiveness and the grace of God. Symbolically, the Sheep Gate denotes the offering of the Lamb, Jesus Christ. Because of the death of Jesus and His shed blood at Calvary, we are redeemed. He paid the ultimate price for the sins of mankind. Jesus Christ is the entrance or door to the Sheep Gate. Jesus Christ can and will save us, transforming us to be in His image. Furthermore, by entering through the Sheep Gate we are offered the gift of salvation upon repentance of our sins through the blood of the Lamb of God. Additionally, the proclamation of the grace of God can be found.

The Sheep Gate is embodied in the redemptive work of the Lord Jesus, who is the door of the sheep. Jesus is the door or gate by which we have access to the Father. Jesus is the way, the truth, and the life; and no man can get to the Father, except through Him.

Therefore, Jesus said again, "Very truly I tell you, I am the gate for the sheep. All who have come before me are thieves and robbers, but the sheep have not listened to them. I am the gate; whoever enters through me will be saved, they will come in and go out, and find pasture. The thief comes only to steal and kill and destroy; I have come that they may have life, and have it to the full. "I am the good shepherd. The good shepherd lays down his life for the sheep. The hired hand is not the shepherd and does not own the sheep. So when he sees the wolf coming, he abandons the sheep and runs away. Then the wolf attacks the flock and scatters it. The man runs away because he is a hired hand and cares nothing for the sheep. I am the good shepherd; I know my sheep and my sheep know me— just as the Father knows me and I know the Father—and I lay down my life for the sheep. I have other sheep that are not of this sheep pen. I must bring them also. They too will listen to my voice, and there shall be one flock and one shepherd. The reason my Father loves me is that I lay down my life—only to take it up again. No one takes it from me, but I lay it down of my own accord. I have authority to lay it down and authority to take it up again. This command I received from my Father.

JOHN 10:7-18 (NIV)

Entering through the Sheep Gate is essential to entry to the kingdom of God, and the choice is ours. You can either choose to have eternal life in heaven by entering through the gate and accepting Christ or choose to reject Him and spend eternity in hell. The death, burial, and resurrection of Jesus provide daily hope for our future, and by becoming a part of the kingdom of God we have hope for eternal life.

> If we say we have no sin [refusing to admit that we are sinners], we delude ourselves and the truth is not in us. [His word does not live in our hearts.] If we [freely] admit that we have sinned and confess our sins, He is faithful and just [true to His own nature and promises], and will forgive our sins and cleanse us continually from all unrighteousness [our wrongdoing, everything not in conformity with His will and purpose]. If we say that we have not sinned [refusing to admit acts of sin], we make Him [out to be] a liar [by contradicting Him] and His word is not in us.
>
> 1 JOHN 1:8-10 (AMP)

We must be converted in addition to being renewed in our way of living and thoughts. Conversion requires us to repent. Repentance is achieved through prayer, as well as by seeking our heavenly Father's forgiveness for all of our wrong thoughts and behavior. Additionally, our conversion must include being water baptized, receiving Christ as our Savior, and the willingness to obey His instructions and live life according to them.

The kingdom of God is extremely important to whom we are to become in Christ. Thus, we have the choice to live with Jesus or in Hell. The choice is ours, wherein the death, burial and resurrection of Jesus provide daily hope for our future. Becoming a part of the kingdom of God, we have hope for eternal life.

FISH GATE

The next gate is the Fish Gate, where fishermen who frequently travelled from the Sea of Galilee brought fish to be sold at the local markets. The Fish Gate is located near Tyre and the Sea of Galilee. The Sea of Galilee is Israel's largest freshwater lake and served as a primary source of drinking water for the nation. It flows into the Jordan River, channeling south into the Dead Sea.

The Fish Gate represents the pathway to eternal life. Jesus taught evangelism to His disciples at the Sea of Galilee, instructing His disciples to be a witness of the glory of the kingdom of God. Jesus promised His disciples that He would make them "fishers of men" if they would follow Him (Matthew 4:19-20). Jesus gave them a promise that would not be broken, and this promise remains today, as we are called to evangelize. He said to them, "Go into all the world and preach the gospel to all creation. Whoever believes and is baptized will be saved, but whoever does not believe will be condemned" (Mark 16:15-16, NIV). Following Jesus provides us with assurance and hope for eternal life, and accepting Him requires us to walk in faith and live according to the fruit of the Holy Spirit.

> But if you are led by the Spirit, you are not under the law. The acts of the flesh are obvious: sexual immorality, impurity and debauchery; idolatry and witchcraft; hatred, discord, jealousy, fits of rage, selfish ambition, dissensions, factions and envy; drunkenness, orgies, and the like. I warn you, as I did before, that those who live like this will not inherit the kingdom of God. But the fruit of the Spirit is love, joy, peace, forbearance, kindness, goodness, faithfulness, gentleness and self-control. Against such things there is no law. Those who belong to Christ Jesus have crucified the flesh with its passions and desires. Since we live by the Spirit, let us keep in step with the Spirit.
>
> GALATIANS 5:18-25 (NIV)

OLD GATE

Following the Fish Gate was the construction of the Old Gate. The Old Gate, also known as the Jeshanah Gate, was built at the northwest corner of Jerusalem. Another name for this gate is the Ephraim Gate. Noteworthy, the Old Gate was built by people who had specific professions.

> So, Christ himself gave the apostles, the prophets, the evangelists, the pastors and teachers, to equip his peo-

ple for works of service, so that the body of Christ may be built up until we all reach unity in the faith and in the knowledge of the Son of God and become mature, attaining to the whole measure of the fullness of Christ. Then we will no longer be infants, tossed back and forth by the waves, and blown here and there by every wind of teaching and by the cunning and craftiness of people in their deceitful scheming. Instead, speaking the truth in love, we will grow to become in every respect the mature body of him who is the head, that is, Christ. From him the whole body, joined and held together by every supporting ligament, grows and builds itself up in love, as each part does its work.

EPHESIANS 4:11-16 (NIV)

This particular gate signifies the death of the "old man." When a person receives Christ, that person's old nature (old man) no longer exists. We no longer should live a life of corruption, deceitfulness, or grudging; and we should not be filled with the hatred that previously existed within us. Redemption renews us in the spirit, in our minds, and in our hearts. We develop and live life with new attitudes and characteristics for daily living in Christ. Redemption brings us to a new existence, demonstrating how we are created after the likeness of God in true righteousness and holiness.

Therefore, having put away falsehood, let each one of you speak the truth with his neighbor, for we are members one of another. Be angry and do not sin; do not let the sun go down on your anger, and give no opportunity to the devil. Let the thief no longer steal, but rather let him labor, doing honest work with his own hands, so that he may have something to share with anyone in need. Let no corrupting talk come out of your mouths, but only such as is good for building up, as fits the occasion, that it may give grace to those who hear. And do not grieve the Holy Spirit of God, by whom you were sealed for the day of redemption. Let all bitterness and wrath and anger and clamor and slander be put away from you, along with all malice. Be kind to one another, tenderhearted, forgiving one another, as God in Christ forgave you.

EPHESIANS 4:25-32 (ESV)

VALLEY GATE

For the Lord your God is bringing you into a good land—a land with brooks, streams, and deep springs gushing out into the valleys and hills; For the Lord your God is bringing you into a good land—a land with brooks, streams, and deep springs gushing out into the valleys and hills;

DEUTERONOMY 8:7 (NIV)

The Valley Gate epitomizes newness of life in Christ and a new way of living through His grace. The Valley Gate, a place of digging deep within ourselves spiritually, represents soul-searching and a pursuit of righteousness. Here's where trusting and living according to the Word of God becomes clear and should be our daily meal. The Valley Gate is a time of purging—ridding ourselves of the evil thoughts and worldly ways and focusing on living in an acceptable manner according to the will of God. The Bible exhorts us to do this in the book of James.

> Know this, my beloved brothers: let every person be quick to hear, slow to speak, slow to anger; for the anger of man does not produce the righteousness of God. Therefore, put away all filthiness and rampant wickedness and receive with meekness the implanted word, which is able to save your souls. But be doers of the word, and not hearers only, deceiving yourselves. For if anyone is a hearer of the word and not a doer, he is like a man who looks intently at his natural face in a mirror. For he looks at himself and goes away and at once forgets what he was like. But the one who looks into the perfect law, the law of liberty, and perseveres, being no hearer who forgets but a doer who acts, he will be blessed in his doing.
>
> JAMES 1:19-25 (ESV)

When a person becomes a new Christian, it is important to allow our new relationship with Christ to guide us. Additionally, traveling through the Valley Gate of our life is a time of realization that we are not alone.

DUNG GATE

Following the erection of the Valley Gate, the Dung Gate was the next gate to come to fruition. The Dung Gate denotes rejection of sin. Healing and deliverance begin with redemption and forgiveness of our sins through the Lord Jesus, laying the foundation for our salvation. The Dung Gate is descriptive of how one's flesh will and must die in order to live a righteous life in Christ. Additionally, the Dung Gate was essentially the gateway to Jerusalem's landfill. It is the gate noted for being the place where waste (trash) was removed to the valley of Hinnom. Hinnom was the location where rubbish was destroyed and burnt. To put it in spiritual terms, the Dung Gate denotes sin and having a bad nature, which destroys the hearts and minds of individuals. In an effort to live a godly life and live holy according to the will of our heavenly Father, we must not have wandering faith but live according to our newfound knowledge and love of Christ.

Spiritually speaking, I was not where I needed to be for a long time. I was at a place and time in my life where I did not allow the totality of my being to become solely submitted to the calling and voice of the Lord. I believe that God allowed me to go through a point in life such as this so that He could get me to the place where He wanted me to be—focused and wholeheartedly committed to Him.

Although God remained in control, I grew weary and very doubtful at one point because of the trials, hardships, heartache, pain, and shame that I endured. A decision had to be made; I had to decide to make up my mind and let God work things out. Baffling as it may be, this is what I missed for so long. I chose the road of many challenges and did not want to accept what I was being prepared for; but after I decided to accept Jesus and make Him the Lord of my life, I went through trials, tribulations, and temptations that propelled me to get T.H.R.O.U.G.H. Entering into a new phase in my life, I am now renewed, recovered, restored, and reconstructed.

FOUNTAIN GATE

The Fountain Gate speaks to us from the source of the Living Water (God as the Holy Spirit). The Fountain Gate is located near the pool of Siloah (Siloam). The name Siloah means sent. This pool is the place where Jesus encountered a blind man who sat poolside daily as many others did, waiting to enter the pool when a healing angel would come and trouble the waters. Because of his impairment the man was looked over and often looked upon as just a mere, insignificant beggar by those who passed by.

> Rabbi, who sinned, this man or his parents, that he was born blind?" Jesus answered, "It was not that this man sinned, or his parents, but that the works of God might be displayed in him. We must work the works of Him who sent me while it is day; night is coming, when no one can work. As long as I am in the world, I am the light of the world." Having said these things, He spit on the ground and made mud with the saliva. Then He anointed the man's eyes with the mud and said to him, "Go, wash in the pool of Siloam" which means Sent. So, he went and washed and came back seeing.
>
> JOHN 9:2-7 (ESV)

Though others may have overlooked this man's state, Jesus did not pass by him without improving his condition. It was at the Fountain Gate that this man received his miracle from the Living Water. The Fountain Gate represents what Jesus teaches in John 7:38: "He that believeth on me, as the scripture hath said, out of his belly shall flow rivers of living water." When we drink from the fountain of the Living Water—its source being Jesus Christ—we will never thirst but live according to His divine purpose.

The Fountain Gate represents holy and pure life in the power of the Holy Spirit. Jesus left the Judean countryside and went back to Galilee, passing through Samaria in the town of Sycar. Having traveled this path for a while, Jesus was tired and thirsty from the journey and sat down to rest at Jacob's well while His disciples went into town seeking food. While resting, Jesus was approached by a Samaritan woman. To the woman's amazement, Jesus spoke to the woman and asked her for a cup of water. By doing this, Jesus broke three Jewish customs: first, he spoke to a woman; second, she was of an ethnic group that the Jews traditionally despised; and third, He asked her to get him a drink of water, which would have made him ceremonially unclean from using her cup or jar. What is noteworthy is that the Samaritan woman was skeptical of Jesus talking to her because of her cultural background and because she was deemed an outcast. As she began to talk with Jesus, she was astonished; but her focus was not on him not drinking. She was more in awe at the fact that Jesus spoke to her. Normally and customarily, Jews had no association with the Samaritans. Jesus assures the woman that everyone who drinks of the water from the well will thirst, but those that drink of the water He gives will not thirst but have everlasting life. Jesus knew her history, yet he accepted her and ministered to her, offering her the living water. As she returned home she shared the experience she had with Jesus. From that day on, many of the people who mocked her became believers in Jesus. The woman at the well set an example of being filled with the Holy Spirit and sharing the good news of Jesus Christ. When we, in spirit and truth, fulfill the desire of our Father to evangelize others and lead them to Him, we can have a monumental impact for the Kingdom. Because of the Samaritan woman's obedience and willingness to spread the word about Jesus, others experienced a spiritual awakening and began to follow Christ (John 4:39-42).

Just as Jesus continued to minister to the woman at the well, He also wants us to be in constant and devoted fellowship and communion with Him on a daily basis. How do we do this? We accomplish this by doing as He instructed the Samaritan woman: worshipping in spirit and in truth.

> And do not get drunk with wine, for that is debauchery, but be filled with the Spirit, addressing one another in psalms and hymns and spiritual songs, singing and making melody to the Lord with your heart,
>
> EPHESIANS 5:18-19 (ESV)

Worshipping in spirit and truth is a two part phenomenon. To worship in spirit means that you commune with God internally with your inner man; and to do it in truth means that your outward attitude of worship is only a reflection of what you inwardly express to God.

WATER GATE

Located next to the Fountain Gate is the Water Gate. Both the Water Gate and the Fountain Gate connect. The Water Gate speaks to us of obedient life in the Holy Spirit. In the Old Testament, water describes the Holy Spirit. Through the Holy Spirit we are made whole, becoming true servants of the Lord through our obedience, love for Christ, and willingness to obey His teachings. Moreover, the Holy Spirit connects with us, bringing life through the Word of God by which we are cleansed, encouraged, and provided with clear directions for our life's journey and the destiny that awaits us.

> And all the people went their way to eat, and to drink, and to send portions, and to make great mirth, because they had understood the words that were declared unto them.
>
> NEHEMIAH 8:12

The book of Nehemiah describes people gathering at the Water Gate to hear the Word of God, instructing Ezra the scribe to bring to them the book of the Law of Moses. The book of the Law of Moses refers to the first five books of the Bible: Genesis, Exodus, Leviticus, Numbers, and Deuteronomy.

> All the people came together as one in the square before the Water Gate. They told Ezra the teacher of the Law to bring out the Book of the Law of Moses, which the Lord had commanded for Israel. So, on the first day of the seventh month Ezra the priest brought the Law before the assembly, which was made up of men and women and all who were able to understand. He read it aloud from daybreak till noon as he faced the square before the Water Gate in the presence of the men, women and others who could understand. And all the people listened attentively to the Book of the Law.
>
> NEHEMIAH 8:1-3 (NIV)

Nehemiah was not just determined to build the gate; he was committed to the spiritual well-being of the people. Nehemiah sought to restore the hope and love for God back to the people. Many years had gone by since the people had last heard the Word of God, and they were humble as they gathered at the Water Gate. The Water Gate was a place where streams of water ran and flowed underground into the city. This stream of water also channeled into the temple of God where the priests bathed. The priests bathed in fresh, running water in order to properly purify themselves to minister to God. The Water Gate was the portion of the city where fresh, living water entered for people to drink and bathe in; and this was where Ezra chose to wash the hearts of God's people by reading the Word of God aloud. The Water Gate was also a place of justice where oaths were taken.

I am the true grapevine, and my Father is the gardener. He cuts off every branch of mine that doesn't produce fruit, and he prunes the branches that do bear fruit, so they will produce even more. You have already been pruned and purified by the message I have given you. Remain in me, and I will remain in you. For a branch cannot produce fruit if it is severed from the vine, and you cannot be fruitful unless you remain in me. "Yes, I am the vine; you are the branches. Those who remain in me, and I in them, will produce much fruit. For apart from me you can do nothing. Anyone who does not remain in me is thrown away like a useless branch and withers. Such branches are gathered into a pile to be burned. But if you remain in me and my words remain in you, you may ask for anything you want, and it will be granted! When you produce much fruit, you are my true disciples. This brings great glory to my Father. "I have loved you even as the Father has loved me. Remain in my love. When you obey my commandments, you remain in my love, just as I obey my Father's commandments and remain in his love. I have told you these things so that you will be filled with my joy. Yes, your joy will overflow! This is my commandment: Love each other in the same way I have loved you. There is no greater love than to lay down one's life for one's friends. You are my friends if you do what I command. I no longer call you slaves, because a master doesn't confide in his slaves. Now you are my friends, since I have told you everything the Father told me. You didn't choose me. I chose you. I appointed you to go and produce lasting fruit, so that the Father will give you whatever you ask for, using my name. This is my command: Love each other.

JOHN 15:1-17 (NLT)

HORSE GATE

The Horse Gate was located on the east side of the city, overlooking the Kidron Valley. The Kidron Valley is constructed between the temple and the garden of Gethsemane. This gate gets its name from the fact that it was located by the horse stables. It was also the gate that Jesus passed through as He made His way to the garden of Gethsemane before His arrest. The Horse Gate is also the place where Judas, who betrayed Christ, hung himself. The spiritual significance of the Horse Gate is that it connotes spiritual warfare.

For we wrestle not against flesh and blood, but against principalities, against powers, against the rulers of the darkness of this world, against spiritual wickedness in high places.

EPHESIANS 6:12

As we live each day, one may find himself or herself in a constant battle for survival. As disciples of Christ, we are guaranteed to come up against spiritual battles because the adversary is always looking for an opportunity to test our faith and belief. As Christians, we are just like soldiers who are battling in a war, except our fight is against Satan and his evil forces. Fighting, even when we already have the victory promised to us, can be difficult. When standing on the promises of the Lord, our battles should not be against each other but side by side with one another, uniting in prayer, studying the Bible together, and encouraging one another. Far too many times, we are engaged in the battle of degrading one another, despite knowing that this displeases God.

But every man is tempted, when he is drawn away of his own lust, and enticed.

JAMES 1:14

God sent His only son to fight the greatest battle ever for us. I have come to a place where greater understanding of the spiritual warfare of the world helps me to find strength even when I think I'm weak. We have the assurance of the Lord that He will fight our battles, and He will arm us with the weapons to destroy what hinders our spiritual being.

> And I saw heaven opened, and behold a white horse; and he that sat upon him was called Faithful and True, and in righteousness he doth judge and make war. His eyes were as a flame of fire, and on his head were many crowns; and he had a name written, that no man knew, but he himself. And he was clothed with a vesture dipped in blood: and his name is called The Word of God. And the armies which were in heaven followed him upon white horses, clothed in fine linen, white and clean. And out of his mouth goeth a sharp sword, that with it he should smite the nations: and he shall rule them with a rod of iron: and he treadeth the winepress of the fierceness and wrath of Almighty God. And he hath on his vesture and on his thigh a name written, KING OF KINGS, AND LORD OF LORDS.
>
> REVELATION 19:11-16

The ultimate fulfilment of the Horse Gate will take place during the Tribulation—the Day of the Lord as described in Revelation 22.

> And, behold, I come quickly; and my reward is with me, to give every man according as his work shall be. I am Alpha and Omega, the beginning and the end, the

first and the last. Blessed are they that do his commandments, that they may have right to the tree of life, and may enter in through the gates into the city. For without are dogs, and sorcerers, and whoremongers, and murderers, and idolaters, and whosoever loveth and maketh a lie. I Jesus have sent mine angel to testify unto you these things in the churches. I am the root and the offspring of David, and the bright and morning star. And the Spirit and the bride say, Come. And let him that heareth say, Come. And let him that is athirst come. And whosoever will, let him take the water of life freely. For I testify unto every man that heareth the words of the prophecy of this book, If any man shall add unto these things, God shall add unto him the plagues that are written in this book: And if any man shall take away from the words of the book of this prophecy, God shall take away his part out of the book of life, and out of the holy city, and from the things which are written in this book.

REVELATION 22:12-19

EAST GATE

The East Gate is located adjacent to the Horse Gate. The East Gate was the first gate to be opened each morning, representing newness of life, glory, and power. Also known as the Beautiful Gate or Golden Gate, the East Gate is one of eight gates built into the walls surrounding the temple mount in Jerusalem which stands facing the Mount of Olives across the Kidron Valley. The Kidron Valley, a place of olive groves, divides Jerusalem's Temple Mount from the Mount of Olives. In contrast to the other gates that comprise the wall, the East Gate is completely sealed shut.

> Then the man brought me back to the outer gate of the sanctuary, the one facing east, and it was shut. The LORD said to me, "This gate is to remain shut. It must not be opened; no one may enter through it. It is to remain shut because the LORD, the God of Israel, has entered through it.
>
> EZEKIEL 44:1–2 (NIV)

The East Gate is the place where the Lord Jesus, the Messiah of Israel, will arrive.

> As Jesus and his disciples approached Jerusalem approaching Bethphage on the Mount of Olives, Jesus sent two disciples.
>
> MATTHEW 21:1 (NIV)

Jesus entered the temple court where people went to pray and witnessed the sacrifices being offered before the holy place. Upon His arrival Jesus entered in dismay as He witnessed the people engaged in selling and buying merchandise. Jesus was saddened by what He saw. He then overturned the tables of the moneychangers and the benches of everyone selling doves, putting an end to the corruption taking place in the temple.

> And Jesus entered the temple [grounds] and drove out [with force] all who were buying and selling [birds and animals for sacrifice] in the temple *area*, and He turned over the tables of the moneychangers [who made a profit exchanging foreign money for temple coinage] and the chairs of those who were selling doves [for sacrifice]. Jesus said to them, "It is written [in Scripture], 'MY HOUSE SHALL BE CALLED A HOUSE OF PRAYER'; but you are making it a ROBBERS' DEN."
>
> MATTHEW 21:12-13 (AMP)

As children of God go through the many spiritual battles that life presents, we are always victorious because of Jesus Christ being our divine Savior. We are assured that Jesus will return one day, and it's up to us to be prepared for His return by living in righteousness, praying, and having fellowship with Him.

> Behold, the day of the Lord cometh, and thy spoil shall be divided in the midst of thee. For I will gather all nations against Jerusalem to battle; and the city shall be taken, and the houses rifled, and the women ravished; and half of the city shall go forth into captivity, and the residue of the people shall not be cut off from the city.

Then shall the Lord go forth, and fight against those nations, as when he fought in the day of battle.

ZECHARIAH 14:1-3

Jesus will return whether you are ready or not. He will return, so make the choice now to follow Him and be prepared.

INSPECTION GATE

The Miphkad Gate or Inspection Gate signifies the judgment of our life and the time when God our Father will separate the believers from the non-believers; it represents the reality check of God summoning everyone for examination. This gate was near the north end of the east wall of Jerusalem and was where King David advised his military commanders prior to battle that someone greater (God) would fight for them.

For we must all appear before the judgment seat of Christ; that everyone may receive the things done in his body, according to that he hath done, whether it be good or bad. Knowing therefore the terror of the Lord, we persuade men; but we are made manifest unto God; and I trust also are made manifest in your consciences. For we commend not ourselves again unto you, but give you occasion to glory on our behalf, that ye may have somewhat to answer them which glory in appearance, and not in heart. For whether we be beside ourselves, it is to God: or whether we be sober, it is for your cause. For the love of Christ constraineth us; because we thus judge, that if one died for all, then were all dead: And that he died for all, that they which live should not henceforth live unto themselves, but unto him which died for them, and rose again. Wherefore henceforth know we no man after the flesh: yea, though we have known Christ after the flesh, yet now henceforth know we him no more. Therefore, if any man be in Christ, he is a new creature: old things are passed away; behold, all things are become new. And all things are of God, who hath reconciled us to himself by Jesus Christ, and hath given to us the ministry of reconciliation; To wit, that God was in Christ, reconciling the world unto himself, not imputing their trespasses unto them; and hath committed unto us the word of reconciliation. Now then we are ambassadors for Christ, as though God did beseech you by us: we pray you in Christ's stead, be ye reconciled to God. For he hath made him to be sin for us, who knew no sin; that we might be made the righteousness of God in him.

2 CORINTHIANS 5:10-21

When the Son of man shall come in his glory, and all the holy angels with him, then shall he sit upon the throne of his glory: And before him shall be gathered all nations: and he shall separate them one from another, as a shepherd divideth his sheep from the

206

goats: And he shall set the sheep on his right hand, but the goats on the left. Then shall the King say unto them on his right hand, Come, ye blessed of my Father, inherit the kingdom prepared for you from the foundation of the world: For I was an hungred, and ye gave me meat: I was thirsty, and ye gave me drink: I was a stranger, and ye took me in: Naked, and ye clothed me: I was sick, and ye visited me: I was in prison, and ye came unto me. Then shall the righteous answer him, saying, Lord, when saw we thee an hungred, and fed thee? or thirsty, and gave thee drink? When saw we thee a stranger, and took thee in? or naked, and clothed thee? Or when saw we thee sick, or in prison, and came unto thee? And the King shall answer and say unto them, Verily I say unto you, Inasmuch as ye have done it unto one of the least of these my brethren, ye have done it unto me. Then shall he say also unto them on the left hand, Depart from me, ye cursed, into everlasting fire, prepared for the devil and his angels: For I was an hungred, and ye gave me no meat: I was thirsty, and ye gave me no drink: I was a stranger, and ye took me not in: naked, and ye clothed me not: sick, and in prison, and ye visited me not. Then shall they also answer him, saying, Lord, when saw we thee an hungred, or athirst, or a stranger, or naked, or sick, or in prison, and did not minister unto thee? Then shall he answer them, saying, Verily I say unto you, Inasmuch as ye did it not to one of the least of these, ye did it not to me. And these shall go away into everlasting punishment: but the righteous into life eternal.

MATTHEW 25:31-46

From here, He will divide all the people who survived the tribulation into two groups: those that will enter His kingdom on earth (the sheep) and those that are to go into everlasting destruction (the goats). The Inspection Gate is the final gate for all believers, and upon the return of Christ we will give an account of our lives unto Him. This will be Judgment day, a day of reckoning with the Lord.

> Now if anyone builds on the foundation with gold, silver, precious stones, wood, hay, straw — each one's work will become manifest, for the Day will disclose it, because it will be revealed by fire, and the fire will test what sort of work each one has done. If the work that anyone has built on the foundation survives, he will receive a reward. If anyone's work is burned up, he will suffer loss, though he himself will be saved, but only as through fire.
>
> 1 CORINTHIANS 3:12-15 (ESV)

The Inspection Gate represents the life that we have lived, in the sense that our life will be revealed before the Lord. Moreover, as we pass through each gate we should seek a relationship that is pleasing and acceptable to God. Nehemiah and those that worked on rebuilding the walls sought others to assist in the completion of each task. As believers and children of God, we must encourage and help lead others through each gate toward the kingdom of God. The apostle Peter reminds us of our call when he said, "As obedient children, not fashioning yourselves according to the former lusts in your ignorance: But as he which hath called you is holy, so be ye holy in all manner of conversation; Because it is written, Be ye holy; for I am holy. And if ye call on the Father, who without respect of persons judgeth according to every man's work, pass the time of your sojourning here in fear" (1 Peter 1:14-17).

Importantly, we must strive to be as sheep that are not scattered, but those that follow the instructions of Christ. We must come together for the kingdom of God—teaching, ministering, uplifting, and seeking to help each other. Why is this important? It's important for our eternal home with the Lord. Goats, on the other hand, do not follow Jesus but wander into the wilderness doing whatever appeals to them.

Jesus begins the parable in Matthew 25 by saying it concerns His glorious return and the establishment of the Kingdom. All those on earth at that time will be brought before the Lord, and He will separate them as a shepherd separates sheep from goats. He will put the sheep on his right and the goats on His left. The sheep on Jesus' right hand are blessed by God the Father and given an inheritance.

As with each gate, there was no insignificant part, but it was the passion and the skillfulness of the people that made the difference. Just as you and I have skills to help each other, we must press toward the Inspection Gate of our lives, determined with the mindset to live righteously so that we will be prepared to live with Jesus Christ forever when He returns. As you approach the Inspection Gate of your life, will you be like redeemed sheep that are saved by grace or the goats that are condemned and lost?

(O)BLIGATION

Obligation is the willingness to go through something for someone else. Have you ever thought of going through something for someone other than yourself? I believe it's what we learn and how we learn to survive, while setting examples according to our faith. Thus, patterned by God's design and charge, the purpose of our life is provided by Him. I have frequently used this expression, "Don't become a part of the problem, become a part of the solution." Funny thing, at one point in my life I could not see anything but problems upon problems. Solutions just did not seem to be in the equation during most of my own trials and tests. I was my own problem.

Blessed is the man who walks not in the counsel of the wicked, nor stands in the way of sinners, nor sits in the seat of scoffers; but his delight is in the law of the LORD, and on his law, he meditates day and night. He is like a tree planted by streams of water that yields its fruit in its season, and its leaf does not wither. In all that he does, he prospers. The wicked are not so, but are like chaff that the wind drives away. Therefore, the wicked will not stand in the judgment, nor sinners in the congregation of the righteous; for the LORD knows the way of the righteous, but the way of the wicked will perish.

PSALM 1 (ESV)

Obligation requires suffering. Was I always willing to suffer? No way! On many occasions, it was just the way things happened. Although Jesus had His reasons for allowing me to go through what I did, I had to reach a place of total commitment. Jesus was no longer accepting a part of me. He wanted all of me. He wanted me to be who He called me to be and what I was born, designed, and intended to be—which is totally committed to Him.

Though pain and endurance come with much heartache, I am learning every day to trust Him more and more to lead the way. Jesus was always showing me who He was. I walked through the valley of despair, time after time. I was afraid, alone, and could not find anyone to stand with me; but a mighty friend was at work in me. I had to let Him in, totally obligating myself to Him, His will, and to living according to His Word. I am changed, I am stronger, and I am chosen to do the will of God. I have become more obligated to help others even amid my storms. I learned to pray for others even when it felt like I'd been mistreated by them and also when it felt like no one cared about what I might be going through. However, I still remained prayerful that God would meet their needs as well as mine. There was a time when I could not pray for anyone else. It was always about my needs. But today, I see greater hope, power, and will in interceding for someone else. Through growth, I found my obligation and commitment to help. Undoubtedly, I have been misused and sometimes abused for helping, but Jesus knows all of that.

As I think about Jesus Christ being a dedicated servant of the Father, I have reached the conclusion that nothing should ever interfere with my or your willingness to help others. We have been created in the image of Christ and must know to whom we belong to while having an attitude of servanthood. The teachings of Jesus illustrate to us the true meaning of loving one another, fellowship, and having a clean heart—which is repentance for any wrongdoing. As true worshippers and believers, there is nothing better than living a life full of the promises of God. God will not deceive you nor give you false hope. Our God *is* and only wants the best for

213

you and me as disciples. As we work and live in righteousness, we must do it according to the will of God because such behavior pleases God and is a blessing to others also. The only hindrance that prevents us from achieving this is our choice to be disobedient to the Lord and His will. Otherwise, Scripture reaffirms to us that what we do for ourselves, we should do for others.

> One of the teachers of the law came and heard them debating. Noticing that Jesus had given them a good answer, he asked him, "Of all the commandments, which is the most important?" "The most important one," answered Jesus, "is this: 'Hear, O Israel: The Lord our God, the Lord is one. Love the Lord your God with all your heart and with all your soul and with all your mind and with all your strength.' The second is this: 'Love your neighbor as yourself.' There is no commandment greater than these." "Well said, teacher," the man replied. "You are right in saying that God is one and there is no other but him. To love him with all your heart, with all your understanding and with all your strength, and to love your neighbor as yourself is more important than all burnt offerings and sacrifices. "When Jesus saw that he had answered wisely, he said to him, "You are not far from the kingdom of God." And from then on no one dared ask him any more questions. One of the teachers of the law came and heard them debating. Noticing that Jesus had given

them a good answer, he asked him, "Of all the commandments, which is the most important?" "The most
important one," answered Jesus, "is this: 'Hear, O Israel: The Lord our God, the Lord is one. Love the Lord
your God with all your heart and with all your soul
and with all your mind and with all your strength.'
The second is this: 'Love your neighbor as yourself.'
There is no commandment greater than these." "Well
said, teacher," the man replied. "You are right in saying that God is one and there is no other but him. To
love him with all your heart, with all your understanding and with all your strength, and to love your
neighbor as yourself is more important than all burnt
offerings and sacrifices." When Jesus saw that he had
answered wisely, he said to him, "You are not far from
the kingdom of God." And from then on no one dared
ask him any more questions.

MARK 12:28-34 (NIV)

Repay no one evil for evil, but give thought to do what
is honorable in the sight of all. If possible, so far as it
depends on you, live peaceably with all. Beloved, never avenge yourselves, but leave it to the wrath of God,
for it is written, "Vengeance is mine, I will repay, says
the Lord." To the contrary, "if your enemy is hungry,
feed him; if he is thirsty, give him something to drink;

for by so doing you will heap burning coals on his head." Do not be overcome by evil, but overcome evil with good.

ROMANS 12:17-21(ESV)

I know, and surely you will know that Satan turns up his game when you are obligated to the Lord by loving Him wholeheartedly and keeping His commandments. God is the divine hope for our future. He promised to never leave us nor forsake us as we go through life.

> Be strong. Take courage. Don't be intimidated. Don't give them a second thought because GOD, your God, is striding ahead of you. He's right there with you. He won't let you down; He won't leave you.
>
> DEUTERONOMY 31:6 (MSG)

I can hear the voice of the Lord saying, "Hold on, my child, I am with you. I will not bring you to a situation or circumstance that you can't handle. I have given you the will power. Now use it to rise above." Enduring the many storms has made the difference for me to this point. My search is over, and now I assuredly know that I belong to the King. There's no second-guessing or wavering about this now. This has been validated through all my struggles, as God has held me in His loving arms and allowed me to share my story with others. Like many of you, I was searching for something and someplace to belong for so very long. I made the choice to stay on this journey that God chose for me. By no means was it easy to make it to the place where I stand today, and it only became harder and harder every step of the way. Clouds of darkness and loneliness, which sometimes blinds us, always seemed to hover over me. Being alone and being let down time after time hurts. I chose to rise above these clouds and discovered that spreading our wings above the clouds brings forth a refreshing river of everlasting and flowing fresh water.

> Come, let us sing for joy to the Lord; let us shout aloud to the Rock of our salvation. Let us come before him with thanksgiving and extol him with music and song. For the Lord is the great God, the great King above all gods. In his hand are the depths of the earth, and the mountain peaks belong to him. The sea is his, for he made it, and his hands formed the dry land. Come, let us bow down in worship, let us kneel before the Lord our Maker; for he is our God and we are the people of his pasture, the flock under his care.
>
> PSALM 95:1-7 (NIV)

I realized that in spite of what I've been through, I did not come through the trials and tests alone—Jesus was there all the time. Jesus was committed to saving me; and all He wants is for me and you to be fully committed to Him. I was so wrapped up in the mess that was happening in my life that I really just got caught up in the web of deception, deceitfulness, fakeness, and illusions of what Satan had me believing. I had to be reminded that God was and is my source of being, not the worldly state we live in. I knew about Jesus and that He died for our sins, but I just was not fully committed. I did not feel the obligation to help anyone when I could not at times seem to help myself. I went to church, I sang in the choir, I joined various church auxiliaries, and I taught Sunday school and vacation Bible school. But had I become fully committed? No! In my mind I knew I wanted to serve the Lord, and I knew it was the right thing to do. However, my heart was saying one thing, and my mind was saying another. I just had to grow up, and I had to get T.H.R.O.U.G.H. by staying in God's way and no other. I needed to build my faith, trust, and dreams on God's promises, not what I thought I could do. I could not do anything alone, nor had I ever. Yet, the devil really made me think I had things; but in reality, I did not have anything alone. God allowed me to do things on my own so that I would in turn seek after Him, especially when I saw that nothing was possible my way. It was all about staying in God's way and preparing for a new day. It was and is all about the will of our Father and no one else. I reached a place where all I wanted to do was surrender my very all to the Lord, but on the other hand, the devil was saying, "Don't surrender. Give in, drink more alcohol and enjoy the high and the lust of your flesh." Truthfully, it felt good, but I knew in my heart that I could no longer walk halfway through life. I had an obligation, a commitment. I realized that God had things He needed me to do, and a decision had to be made. I had to give up the things that prevented me from fulfilling the will of the Father and reaching my true calling.

Life is to be enjoyed because it is a gift from God. Trials will surely come, and going through them is only a tool that causes you to seek after the Lord even more — not just to get you through, but to make you a total and completely committed servant and obligated to being an advocate of the Lord. At times, my choice was to not look up to the Father; and often, more than I would like to admit, it resulted in more tears and wallowing in greater sorrow. On my journey to being committed, I am blessed in the fact that some time ago I acquired a love for gospel music. I had to learn to sing and praise God during situations. Singing and listening to the music stirred up something within me so much that sometimes I just could not just shake the feeling away; and I was compelled to praise God in music and song as the Bible implores us (See Psalm 95:2).

Now, I am changed within; and Jesus changed my life completely, turning me around so that I could see more of His love and lead others to His love and glory by virtue of the tests that I had to endure. You may say now, "Well, how will I lead one to God's love?" Just look at me. I am what you may call a true "living testimony" of His glory. Jesus did it, not Pat, but Jesus. He changed my life! The key to pointing others to God's love is by being a living, walking testimony for Him. Let your life be an example to those who need to see His love in action.

Although I had continued to attend church regularly, it wasn't until my life became totally changed that I realized how profound a factor that church could be to one's existence. I began to appreciate it more and gained better understanding for the Word of God. I felt more love in my heart even though I was betrayed or mistreated by many people. When others mistreat me now, I can walk away smiling rather than react angrily. I may not display this level of maturity and unconditional love all the time because I am still being groomed and matured for Kingdom building. But let me assure you, my hurt no longer lasts forever like it used to. This change has made me happy and invoked me to help others find this same joy. I have renewed faith, the faith my mother spoke to me about early in my young adult life. I once viewed my faith as something unknown and strange, almost to the point I denied it. I have learned to forgive, when in earlier years forgiveness was impossible. Mainly, this change—the change in my attitude, my thinking and the way I made the decision to live—is all because I found a wonderful true friend, Jesus Christ. He's everything and I look forward to living with Him for eternity. I have become changed from my old sinful ways; I no longer walk in shame but in the brightness and fruitfulness of love that was sacrificed for me.

Truthfully, God will make the change in your life as well. Assessing my commitment to Christ was not easy, and it required me to go through some things—hurt, pain, and sorrow. However, the victory at the end—knowing God still cares and heals the brokenhearted—made it worthwhile. Commit yourself to His ways and His will, and you will not be sorry in the end either. The rewards will definitely outweigh the labor.

The preparations of the heart in man, and the answer of the tongue, is from the Lord. All the ways of a man are clean in his own eyes; but the Lord weigheth the spirits. Commit thy works unto the Lord, and thy thoughts shall be established. The Lord hath made all things for himself: yea, even the wicked for the day of evil. Every one that is proud in heart is an abomination to the Lord: though hand join in hand, he shall not be unpunished. By mercy and truth iniquity is purged:

221

and by the fear of the Lord men depart from evil. When a man's ways please the Lord, he maketh even his enemies to be at peace with him. Better is a little with righteousness than great revenues without right. A man's heart deviseth his way: but the Lord directeth his steps.

PROVERBS 16:1-9

God really cares about you and what you are facing. Commit yourself to Him and watch Him guide, comfort, and lead you to a place of peace, joy, and happiness that nothing or no one else can provide. I encourage you to be committed in every aspect of your life; and I encourage you to walk in faith, hope, and God's love. Shouting "Hallelujah!" has new meaning for me now, and I praise God for how He has brought me through. I am so committed to Him, and I can't thank Him enough. I will continue to thank Him as I can now lift my voice and hands to rejoice always in His grace and mercy. When I think of what the Lord has done for me and meant to me because of my commitment to Him, I can't help but think of the song "Tis So Sweet to Trust in Jesus." I thank the Lord for saving me and for all He's done for me!

(U)NDERSTANDING ASSIGNMENTS: WARFARE

Trust in the Lord with all your heart, And lean not on your own understanding; In all your ways acknowledge Him, And He shall direct your paths. Do not be wise in your own eyes; Fear the Lord and depart from evil. It will be health to your flesh, And strength to your bones. Honor the Lord with your possessions, And with the firstfruits of all your increase;

PROVERBS 3:5-9 (NKJV)

As we journey through life, our paths change; and each day brings us to the dawn of a new day. As the transitioning days give way to changing seasons, our life's journey should be fully committed to the Lord, and that should never change.

As our lives go through its various vicissitudes, we must understand that we will endure spiritual warfare at certain stages along the way. Every child of God will surely engage in spiritual warfare at some point in life. The adversary (Satan) knows what God has in store for His children, so he fights to keep us unfocused on the good things such as thoughts of love, joy, peace, and happiness. By gaining control of our inner thoughts, Satan will cause us to resort to negative actions and be disobedient to the Father. Is Satan at work on your thoughts, ways, and actions? Okay, maybe not now, but he will make every attempt to trick you as you look up to the Lord God. Spiritual battles challenge each of us every day; and learning to deal with and handle our spiritual warfare is essential to our maturity in Christ.

One of Satan's key strategic plots is to attack our minds. By being cognizant of the enemy's attacks and reminding ourselves that God calls us to renew our minds daily, we will be able to discern exactly whose voice we hear and where it is coming from. Spiritual battles and warfare are real, and that's why we must first assess ourselves and our current state of being. Knowing who we are and who we are destined to be will give us the strength and determination to fight the battles so we can become stronger in our fight and continue to stand on the Word of God.

One thing that is of great importance when engaging in spiritual battle is to understand how these battles are fought, how the adversary attacks, and how we can control it instead of letting it control us. As we struggle with issues and situations, we often feel like giving up, and I can certainly attest to the fact that I had that thought. Satan's primary objective is to make us give in and quit. I almost gave up on writing this book several times; and my battles and my struggle to write never seemed to cease. As the attacks continued while I was writing, I heard in the back of my mind: "Who cares about what you've been through? Who would even care about you? You have nothing to offer, and nothing will ever come out of this." Though I was under duress and heavy attack, I refused to give in to the enemy's tricks. In case you haven't noticed yet, I *was* able to complete this book!

For a while now, one of my dreams has been to meet Bishop T.D. Jakes and Joyce Meyers. In 1997, I attended the Woman Thou Art Loosed conference, and I was very excited about going to a conference that would forever change my life. Most assuredly, it really did change my life! I remember the many women walking all over the building, women of different nationalities and walks of life. Prior to the doors opening for the service each day, women would stand outside and gather in song and praise, just thanking God for allowing each of us to come together for such a time; and it did not matter who you knew or who you did not know. There was no doubt that God was opening many doors. On one particular night of the conference, I remember just looking up into the high ceiling and staring into the bright, luminous lights— funny how the brightness did not hurt my eyes. I began to see unimaginable things. I never uttered a word, but I could not wait to get home to call my mother. Spiritually, in the lights I could see the following: the car that I needed parked in my driveway; the husband I wanted, standing by my side; healing; and deliverance. At that moment God began to give me utterance (speaking in unknown tongues) like I had never experienced before. I was refreshed, renewed, and full of excitement; and as I told the story to others, I was overwhelmed with joy. When giving my mother a recap of my experience, she said that I would get the chance to shake Bishop Jakes' hand. Although, it has not happened thus far, I am counting on it happening someday. Why, you ask? Well, shortly after attending the conference I did get the car, I got married soon, I was healed, I had a successful surgery, and I was delivered from what had me bound.

Once upon a time I really did not care to watch Joyce Myers because she just did not hold my interest. I had heard all about her books and conferences, but one day the phrase, "battlefield of the mind," started ringing in my ears. I kept hearing this endlessly. *Now, what is this all about?* I thought. This phrase would not go away, and it just continuously pierced my inner being. Eventually, I began to watch Joyce Myers' broadcasts, and amazingly, I was so drawn to them that from that point on I began watching her every week. I discovered that her teaching not only had a great impact on my thoughts and development process, but it was also empowering for women in general.

I began to have aspirations to attend the conferences she held, and I also wanted to meet her and ask her questions. Interestingly, as I watched the show at times, it was as though she knew my thoughts as she often made statements that addressed what I was thinking. I observed the reactions of the many women who sat attentively in the audience and listened to her speak. *Oh my,* I thought. *She's awesome, I want to go to a conference, and I want to meet her.* And so, one day I sat thinking of how it would be to meet this woman of God. One day, while scrolling through Facebook, it was to my surprise that Joyce Myers wanted to be friends with me! I was so excited, and I could not wait to get to work to tell everyone who my new friend was.

Meeting Joyce Myers and Bishop Jakes is clearly in view. Needless to say, I would love to meet a few others such as Oprah Winfrey and Michelle and Barrack Obama. This may seem absurd in some respects, but nothing is impossible if you believe.

> And the Lord said, "Indeed the people are one and they all have one language, and this is what they begin to do; now nothing that they propose to do will be withheld from them.
>
> GENESIS 11:6 (NKJV)

As I grew closer to the Lord and let the Holy Spirit become my guide, my faith began to grow and so did my will to serve the Lord. I often hear people say "put away self," but I didn't understand this until I arrived at getting T.H.R.O.U.G.H. Putting away self meant that I had to get rid of my old ways and habits, fear, and doubt. Undeniably, it also meant putting Christ first—putting nothing or no one before Him—and first always. Additionally, placing the will and desire of Christ at the forefront of my heart and mind gave new meaning to my daily walk. I had to believe within myself that something greater lay ahead for me even when I continued to go through what I went through. And now, I can proudly present and introduce myself as a born-again, renewed witness of Christ. I stand as a witness today to celebrate the wonders and greatness of Christ. God has equipped me with everything that I need to win and overcome any battle that I encounter. Today, I am standing and living by faith, in hope, and surely in God's love as a victorious overcomer. As recorded in the book of Colossians:

> But now you must also rid yourselves of all such things as these: anger, rage, malice, slander, and filthy language from your lips. Do not lie to each other, since you have taken off your old self with its practices and have put on the new self, which is being renewed in knowledge in the image of its Creator. Here there is no Gentile or Jew, circumcised or uncircumcised, barbarian, Scythian, slave or free, but Christ is all, and is in all. Therefore, as God's chosen people, holy and dearly loved, clothe yourselves with compassion, kindness, humility, gentleness and patience. Bear with each other and forgive one another if any of you has a grievance against someone. Forgive as the Lord forgave you.
>
> COLOSSIANS 3:8-13 (NIV)

The renewed version of me can no longer hold the anger or pain from the past. My assignment was clear—it was now time to move on and change the course I was previously on. It was a new day, a new way, and a new life. The battles we face in life are especially more difficult when we accept Christ as our Savior. Our acceptance, repentance, and water baptism will cause us to lose friends and family relationships. Few earthly relationships, I believe, are life-lasting. As we grow in Christ and become closer to Him, those that are still walking by the flesh instead of by faith will not understand; and the adversary will try to use them to deter us from our destiny.

People will not always understand the newness I've have found, but I will strive to help the sick, brokenhearted, wounded, and even the haters know one thing for sure: Jesus is real! Not everyone will stop focusing on the old person that you once were in lieu of celebrating the new you. Focusing on the old you will continue to be the topic for many who live outside the will of God, but the Word of God offers us encouragement as it pertains to this scenario.

> If the world hate you, ye know that it hated me before it hated you. If ye were of the world, the world would love his own: but because ye are not of the world, but I have chosen you out of the world, therefore the world hateth you. Remember the word that I said unto you, The servant is not greater than his lord. If they have persecuted me, they will also persecute you; if they have kept my saying, they will keep yours also. But all these things will they do unto you for my name's sake, because they know not him that sent me.
>
> JOHN 15:18-21

Withstanding persecution brings forth our ability to gain knowledge and understanding of our calling and assignments. For many years, as I began to grow in Christ, the unction to do more for God started to surface in my feelings and thoughts. I began to have a stronger desire to work in the church. Working in church and being of service to others has helped me grow to become a strong and passionate woman for Christ. As I pressed forward and applied myself to serve more, obstacles would arise, but because of my purpose they were insignificant and inconsequential. I refused to let anything prevent me from doing all that I could do for God.

> And into whatsoever city or town ye shall enter, enquire who in it is worthy; and there abide till ye go thence. And when ye come into an house, salute it. And if the house be worthy, let your peace come upon it: but if it be not worthy, let your peace return to you. And whosoever shall not receive you, nor hear your words, when ye depart out of that house or city, shake off the dust of your feet. Verily I say unto you, It shall be more tolerable for the land of Sodom and Gomorrha in the day of judgment, than for that city. Behold, I send you forth as sheep in the midst of wolves: be ye therefore wise as serpents, and harmless as doves. But beware of men: for they will deliver you up to the councils, and they will scourge you in their synagogues; And ye shall be brought before governors

and kings for my sake, for a testimony against them and the Gentiles.

MATTHEW 10:11-18

Here's where understanding who we are and what our purpose is makes the difference. God calls His children to be Kingdom builders. As Kingdom builders, we are required to work on ourselves and help others too. Had I not gone through the trials and tests that I went through, I would not be of help to others going through similar ordeals. I was pushed to the point where I had to seek God in every way possible. There were times I cried to the point where my tear ducts were completely dry and no more water could possibly stream down my face; but I was still crying internally. What was key for me was learning to apply Scripture in order to meet the demands of my heart and thoughts. I had to believe it and quote it as a melody in my heart. The Word kept my mind and body from succumbing to temptation. As a result of my spiritual warfare, I now understand that God was calling me to be His servant. I had to go T.H.R.O.U.G.H. to get through the warfare, finding strength and hope to live and work in a way that was pleasing to God. I understand my assignment, and I understand now what warfare means. I'm really getting myself together. I had to focus on who I was born to be, not what I had gone through or what the devil attempted to make me into.

My assignment (as well as everyone else's) in life is to desire to be in a relationship with our heavenly Father. There were so many times I sought relationships with people without seeking the Lord first and just functioned according to my perception, senses, and desires. Though there have been several unsuccessful relationships in my life, nothing compares to the relationship I now have with my heavenly Father. To me, understanding warfare meant that I had to pray for myself and others and teach others to pray and believe in what they were praying for just as Jesus taught the disciples.

> Pray then like this: "Our Father in heaven, hallowed be your name. Your kingdom come, your will be done, on earth as it is in heaven. Give us this day our daily bread, and forgive us our debts, as we also have forgiven our debtors. And lead us not into temptation, but deliver us from evil. For if you forgive others their trespasses, your heavenly Father will also forgive you,
>
> MATTHEW 6:9-14 (ESV)

Living according to the will of God brings us to eternal life. As life directs us to many courses throughout our journey, we all have an assignment. Jesus had an assignment and followed the will of the Father. His assignment entailed being beaten, scorned, mocked, and abused. Do you know and are you sure of what your assignment is? Are you listening to the voice of the Lord? I was so broken that many times it felt like nothing would ever come my way, or I wouldn't get to know the Lord as the Light of the World. We are blessed in the fact that we have a true friend.

> Then spake Jesus again unto them, saying, I am the light of the world: he that followeth me shall not walk in darkness, but shall have the light of life.
>
> JOHN 8:12

As we allow the light of Christ to shine upon all of our ways and learn to erase our fears and doubts, we must also allow the power of the Holy Spirit to reside within us. Jesus walked consistently in the power of the Spirit because of His prayer life.

> And in the morning, rising up a great while before day, he went out, and departed into a solitary place, and there prayed.
>
> MARK 1:35

The first task of our daily regimen should be a conversation with the Lord. There are approximately 250 references to prayer throughout the Bible letting us know that it is critical and vital for us to communicate with the Father on a daily basis. Our conversations with Him should consist of thanksgiving, confession, and worship. Making this our daily priority expresses our obedience to

Him. We must do as the Word of God tells us: "Rejoice evermore. Pray without ceasing. In everything give thanks: for this is the will of God in Christ Jesus concerning you" (1 Thessalonians 5:16-18). Prayer is critical if you are going to survive spiritual warfare and accomplish our assignment.

(G)IRDING UP OUR LOINS

As Christians, we must be firmly rooted to live by the truth. Furthermore, it is of utmost importance that we always remain anchored in the Word of God. The devil's tactics are cunning, deceptive, and can appear to be smooth. Psalm 119:105 notes that the Word is a lamp to guide our feet and a light for our paths. Christ must be the priority for our daily living. The benefit of equipping ourselves in the Word of God and keeping His commandments is that we are strengthened for the obstacles, difficulties, and life issues that arise. The Word of God helps gird us for what's to come in the days and nights that lay ahead.

Girding myself for life's battle meant that I had to go through the battle, significantly believing in myself as an overcomer. I had to find and believe that I could make it through. There have been times when I was extremely unprepared for my battles; but in overcoming the many battles of my life, I give all credit to Jesus for bringing me through them. This meant my total being had to be truly, and in the sincerest way, committed and anchored while holding firm to my love for God and trusting Him even more. Satan made strong advances; but I thank God for sustaining me, for He is stronger than the adversary and arose from the grave with all power. I thank God for His love and power that are like no other.

When storms arise and everything seems to be falling apart, don't give up the fight. Continue to fight your battle. Believe and declare victory in the name of Jesus. Always know and believe that the victory is a sweet smell and the beginning of a new walk and talk. Victory is also your destiny calling you to rise above. Life may have presented you with many challenges and at times even felt like an army chasing and holding you back. Surely, you have experienced feelings of being trapped or frightened much like I have; but in life, the hard times elevated you to a place of renewed strength and a desire to fight on. I knew that the battle wasn't over. I knew that I had to march on through life like a solider going to battle. Learning this lesson was hard, and I really had to fight for my life and the life of my unsaved children and family. I knew that God controlled my destiny; God, my

Father in heaven, controls all our fates. To receive deliverance, I learned that I had to stand in the midst of the storm— the tests and trials that I had to go through to receive my healing and become who God designed me to be. I had to be who God intended for me to become and not who I wanted to be.

As I was tossed to and fro by the north winds, it felt like the wind blew harder and harder, sometimes almost causing me to fall to the ground—not really a bad thing because then I could kneel and pray on bended knees. I was continuously pushed and shoved, and in some instances, all I could do was let the storm's winds blow as they did from the north to the south. One thing to note is that the north wind is the strongest wind—it causes things to change, shift, and move around. Spiritually speaking, its movement removes our past sins, ungodly behavior, and any manner that is not of God. The north wind sweeps hard and long. The north wind is biblically referred to as the wind of transition. It signifies the opening of new chapters, and it also denotes the closing of chapters and periods of time.

> The north wind driveth away rain: so doth an angry
> countenance a backbiting tongue.
>
> PROVERBS 25:23

During the era of Samuel, the north winds were propelling, meaning that Israel's rule was transitioning from the era of the judges to that of kings. Additionally, the north wind suggests "revival time" or the springing forth of some sort of renewal. In the natural, north winds signify the transition from one season to the next. Spiritually, revival time implies that the presence of God is coming upon the horizon.

> And I looked, and, behold, a whirlwind came out of the north, a great cloud, and a fire infolding itself, and a brightness was about it, and out of the midst thereof as the colour of amber, out of the midst of the fire.
>
> EZEKIEL 1:4

> Be glad then, ye children of Zion, and rejoice in the Lord your God: for he hath given you the former rain moderately, and he will cause to come down for you the rain, the former rain, and the latter rain in the first month.
>
> JOEL 2:23

The wind seemed silent; there was no howling or tree limbs swaying from side to side, but it was obvious and evident that something was happening in my life. There was a noticeable shift—a shift indicating the change that my life was on a different course and I was closer to my destiny, calling, and God's purpose for my life. In a clear line of sight was a new day, a new beginning, and new way of doing things; things would never be the same. God had forgiven me of my wrongdoing; and He healed my broken heart and restored my mind. The winds may have tossed me all around, but life was moving in a way in which my victory could only be granted by the grace of God. I had a calling to fulfill; I had *Will Power: The Call to Rise Above* on the inside of me. Now, I could rise above and beyond my circumstances and situations.

In spite of all of this the adversary knew my destiny and proceeded to tempt me; but with God on my side and as I arrived to answer His calling, my destiny was all I could and can see now. Through the tests and trials, I had to learn the meaning of "girding" one's self. What I apprehended was that through prayer and belief in God's Word, I could gird myself and weather whatever storm I had to endure. I had to become anchored in the Word of God and in my faith. As I matured in life, I grew and am still growing more and more in love with Christ. I need more of Jesus every day, much like we all do. Growing in communion and fellowship with Christ day after day is totally transformative and presents you with prolific life that only Jesus can give.

The thief cometh not, but for to steal, and to kill, and to destroy: I am come that they might have life, and that they might have it more abundantly.

JOHN 10:10

Jesus promised to give us life and abundant life at that. Even though I have to deal with jealousy, disappointment, hurt, and pain at times, I am still standing on the promises of God. I have many dreams, goals, and hopes in my view. I can see clearly that God is my hope, my strength, and everything I need. Nothing—no storm, dilemma, hardship, or circumstance—will ever come between me and my love and desire to serve the Lord. He is greater than any situation or problem that we face, and He is sovereign—having reign and rule over everything.

Because of what Jesus did for me when He died on the cross, it is my mindset to go all the way with Him without having any reservations about what I'm going through or what I went through in the past. I am no longer holding on to the unwelcomed feelings of hurt, shame, and despair. I'm now holding on to the precious love and gifts of God, things that no man can ever take away. Though the winds shift and toss me around at times, all I can see is God's love for me and the love I have for Him in return. Holding on to God and His amazing and wonderful grace makes life so rich, fruitful, and awesome. I have girded myself with the truth that lies within my heart, the breastplate of righteousness, true love, and fellowship with the Lord who created the heavens and the earth.

> Finally, my brethren, be strong in the Lord, and in the power of his might. Put on the whole armour of God, that ye may be able to stand against the wiles of the devil. For we wrestle not against flesh and blood, but against principalities, against powers, against the rulers of the darkness of this world, against spiritual wickedness in high places. Wherefore take unto you the whole armour of God, that ye may be able to withstand in the evil day, and having done all, to stand. Stand therefore, having your loins girt about with truth, and having on the breastplate of righteousness; And your feet shod with the preparation of the gospel of peace; Above all, taking the shield of faith, wherewith ye shall be able to quench all the fiery darts of the wicked. And take the helmet of salvation, and the sword of the Spirit, which is the word of God:
>
> EPHESIANS 6:10-17

God's love and provision help us to be leaders, be teachers, and set examples for others. When in doubt, we have inspiration provided by the Holy Spirt to gird us up, lead us, and guide us in our way of living and teaching.

(H)EALING:

THE ART OF PATIENCE

Most times, I have the desire and passion to help others. I come from a family that was known throughout the city and state for participating in community programs, political support groups, and various church events. At a very early age, I began getting involved in public service and church. Most of the time I truly thought that I was doing what my parents wanted me to do because *they* were always involved certain activities. However, it wasn't until much later in my life that I realized that my early involvement in such activities was training and discipline for Kingdom building, leadership, and stewardship.

Throughout my lifetime, I have acquired knowledge and instructions as I meet people from different professions or trades, frequently resulting in life-lasting relationships and the acquisition of new skills. I have been afforded the great opportunity to learn and develop a wealth of wisdom from these relationships, which have enabled me to assist many others by matching my skills to their needs. Amazingly, many people have sought my help for education, available resources, survival guidance, or support when facing a crisis stemming from family matters. I have been involved in several Bible study groups, conferences, strategic planning courses, and more. However, there were many times I really did not understand this because I had dealt with so much of my own dilemmas. For a while, I wondered why anyone would want me to help them. Here's where I allowed doubt to have a major role in my thinking and belief. I was at a place where I was challenged each day and unable to see that God had a plan for me. I was ignorant of the fact that God was allowing me to go through and had plans for my survival. Trusting and believing in God truly work wonders when we apply it to our circumstances. Moreover, we must learn to step aside to let God handle our troubles and stop trying to do what only He can do. As we go through life, one thing that we must be assured of is that God does have a plan for each and every one of us. God does love us and want His children to live a good life.

> For God so loved the world that he gave his one and only Son, that whoever believes in him shall not perish but have eternal life.
>
> JOHN 3:16 (NIV)

His love is perfect, unconditional, and available to all. That's pure love for everyone—love which is unforgettable. God did not promise us that we would face days free from pain, sadness, or unsolvable issues. Our efforts to fulfill His plans will be challenging and hard at times, with bittersweet days. Our relationship with the Lord guides us when we totally surrender and open our hearts and minds to His voice. Therefore, the commitment and willfulness to be the vessel that we were designed to be is a significant choice we must make. You can either choose to live according to God's Word or live in disobedience, ignorance, and love for the ways of the world, which will result in eternity in the lake of fire known as hell.

It is when we become dedicated and committed to God that our very existence and who we are destined to be become acceptable to Him. When we devote our lives to help others in the ways of the Lord, nothing is impossible. On the other hand, if we do not, life just becomes more of a challenge in which the adversary deters us from the will of God. Therefore, more will be required—more work and time to develop our true calling. Proverbs 3:27 provides the following instruction: "Do not withhold good from those to whom it is due, when it is in your power to do it" (ESV). In accordance to God's Word, we are to help those in need. In our giving, we should perform the task at hand with genuine love and compassion for others, not just because it's the right thing to do, but because it is pleasing to our heavenly Father. Helping others requires much faith, hope, and compassion; and we should become better equipped by studying and abiding by God's Word.

Healing—whether it's individual or by assisting others with their own healing process—requires daily devotion and conversation with the Lord. It is not just mandatory for special occasions or in moments of distress; but we must and should frequently study and pray, praying for each other just as we pray for ourselves.

Although life has its highs and lows, we must be grateful for life because Jesus died so that we may have life and that more abundantly. There have been many that have never had the chance to experience the life that we live. Some never make it past infancy, while others have had their lives cut short by unforeseen circumstances. I can remember the birth of my first child and the excitement that flowed throughout my family. Even though there was much excitement at his birth, there was just as much sorrow several years later because of his early death at the age of thirteen from a drowning accident. My son was an avid attendee of Sunday school, and he was well on his way to leading others to attend Sunday school—rapidly becoming one of the popular youths in the community for doing so. In spite of his early death, helping others is truly what he is remembered for doing.

I'm reminded of a song I heard him singing; worldly as it was, it had real meaning to him and would later have a greater meaning to me. Tyrone could be seen standing tall and smiling; he was always happy, and he would bellow out the words of the song, "Ain't No Stoppin' Us Now." Tyrone did not believe that anything could stop his dreams, his family life, and more importantly, his fellowship with and love for the Lord. Tyrone was baptized at an early age; and some even spoke of him as being "the little preacher." He loved life, loved people, and always found a way to be surrounded by a group of people. On the day of his death, he forewarned family members to find someone to be with on that day. Sadly, his body was found shortly thereafter at the bottom of a nearby river where he lay motionless after drowning while being caught by an undercurrent while swimming. Though his life was unfortunately truncated, Tyrone maximized the time that he had here on earth and left an impact. It is imperative that we do the same by allowing ourselves to go through the healing process and helping others heal also.

God, our heavenly Father, watches over us night and day; and He truly hears our crying hearts and knows our thoughts. God is always working, but sometimes it's just that our focus is on the wrong thing. Learning from what we go through and finding comfort in God are steps in the direction of being prepared by God for our assignments. God is busy preparing you and me! I thank God for His progressive work in my life.

> Yea, though I walk through the valley of the shadow of death, I will fear no evil: for thou art with me; thy rod and thy staff they comfort me.
>
> PSALM 23:4

God is our comforter, hope, and existence. As I began to reflect on the many times I offered and provided my help to others, a part of me was saying, "How come?" I could hear the voice of the adversary saying, "They are just using you because of what and who you know or knew." During many situations, I became weary, tired, and heartbroken; I was often sad and lacked support from my so-called friends or family whenever I reached out to them. Gratefully, because of whom God designed me to be, I later learned that He had a real purpose for me through my willingness to be obedient to Him. I still did and will do whatever is possible to help others. Let's not get the story misconstrued—yes, I will aid those that I can, now that I have been blessed to discern the phoniness of haters and those who freeload and poach to get whatever they can get out of me for their own selfish gain.

I now understand why I felt hurt and disappointed so many times. I had not convinced myself completely that all I was doing was what God provided me the wisdom to do. I was not allowing God to use me for His glory. I was allowing myself to predict and become empowered by what I was able to achieve and by what I could do to please others. Sure, God provided me with the wisdom, experience, and people to share my knowledge with; but He also blessed me with the warmth and tenderness to help others so that it would be pleasing to Him—all for His glory and not mine. Previously, I had always made everything about me, due to my "stinking thinking" mindset. I'm sure you've done the same thing before too, so let's not think or act as though we haven't seen this done before. We all make mistakes, and at some point we all have taken things for granted. From my mistakes, I have learned to seek the Lord first before I do anything.

And Jesus answered him, The first of all the commandments is, Hear, O Israel; The Lord our God is one Lord: And thou shalt love the Lord thy God with all thy heart, and with all thy soul, and with all thy mind, and with all thy strength: this is the first commandment. And the second is like, namely this, Thou shalt love thy neighbor as thyself. There is none other commandment greater than these.

MARK 12:29-31

When we learn to appreciate who we are in Christ and live according to His will, our divine destiny of helping others becomes a part of whom we were made to be. As Kingdom builders, we set examples by our godly living and by walking in faith, hope, and God's love. Living holy in every way, giving service to those in need, and striving for greatness are pleasing to our heavenly Father. After becoming aware of this concept, the "stinking thinking" arose once again in my mind, but lying above those thoughts was the truth that God called me to be His servant. Just as Jesus and His disciples went about Kingdom business—teaching and helping others—they too suffered. Contrary to their suffering, my suffering was due in part to me not putting Christ first. I created and allowed my thoughts to become twisted by what I was not seeing. In many instances when I helped someone and provided them with a much needed resource, that would be the end of it—no more contact from the individual and they would act as though they didn't know me anymore. I struggled with that for a while, but now I must laugh because it's their struggle, not mine. I'm free! On many occasions, this wasn't just happening at work, school, or in the community. It was happening in church as well, at the hands of those who uttered the praises of God. Amazing how the same people who gained from what I could offer couldn't even say "thank you" or pray that my gift for aiding others would be strengthened. Many people who I believed to be true Christians were the main ones who turned their backs on me. How thankful I am to God that He smiled down upon me and did not let me forget His love. No doubt I was disheartened, but I continued to help and am still willing to be of service. My compassion, even for those that have taken advantage of my help, has not changed. What has changed is my desire to increase in service and help others gain the tools and compassion to freely aid others as well. Jesus paid the price years ago. There is no need for us to put a price tag on our service.

I honestly believe that people will make more and more demands for my help; but I am at a point in time where I openly invite people to ask for help because I can now share the Word of God and be a witness of my struggles and how God saved and delivered me from the heartaches, struggles, and the storm winds that blew across my path. People will be who they think they are until true revelation happens, and that's when they learn their identity, purpose, and destiny to live according God's will. Through it all, the results of our life lessons and experiences should be for God's glory and not ours.

If you were to look in a hypothetical mirror, what would you see? Who would you see? Would you see the love of God and His purpose for you? Or are you only seeing yourself and what you desire to be? Here's where I fell short. I was in a mess, and I was looking at the wrong picture. I was the one who was in control of my life. I made the decisions. I chose to say *yes* to situations before seeking the Lord in my attempt to do well and help others. Guilty I was, and admitting it sometimes makes me cognizant of the guilt all over again. We all have been there at some point in our lives. Praise the Lord! I became better in my walk and talk with the Lord. My worship is with the Lord, not mankind. Now when I teeter on the verge of slipping back into controlling things like I used to, God steps in every time and re-minds me to let Him drive. The more I hear and listen to His voice each day, the less burdensome my decision-making becomes. Can we resolve every situation or cir-cumstance that occurs? The answer is found in the book of Matthew:

As evening approached, the disciples came to Him and said, "This is a remote place, and it's already getting late. Send the crowds away, so they can go to the villages and buy themselves some food."

MATTHEW 14:15 (NIV)

What can we do alone? What can we do to help others? Can we pay the debt we owe to the Lord by engaging in acts of service for the kingdom of God? Can we charge for what has already been paid? Jesus paid the price on the cross for everything mankind would ever owe. Resting on His shoulders as He was led to the cross was our guilt, humiliation, agony, torment, feeling of abandonment, and loneliness. He felt separated from the Father, as He could no longer feel God's presence. He drew His final breath, and His cry of surrender was heard in the midst of the darkness.

For whether we be beside ourselves, it is to God: or whether we be sober, it is for your cause. For the love of Christ constraineth us; because we thus judge, that if one died for all, then were all dead: And that he died for all, that they which live should not henceforth live unto themselves, but unto him which died for them, and rose again. Wherefore henceforth know we no man after the flesh: yea, though we have known Christ after the flesh, yet now henceforth know we him no more.

2 CORINTHIANS 5:13-16

Reflect now on a time when you have been very hurt—maybe you stepped on a nail or cut yourself; maybe you felt shame, humiliation, or insult; maybe you were laughed at or even felt neglected. Yet, the grief we may have felt during our lifetime will never, nor can it, compare to those feelings Jesus felt as He experienced the torture and agony of being crucified. Can you even imagine when you prayed time and time again, but your medical report still came back negative? Perhaps, you've been praying, but depression takes residence within you. Maybe you even lost a longtime friendship or relationship with someone. What then do you do when you keep praying and you can't seem to hear the voice of the Lord nor feel the presence of the Holy Spirit within you? What then do you do when you must walk alone or feel like you're bearing your burden alone? Look to the Lord our Savior and just keep looking to Him. In the book of Revelation, we find the names of our Lord as being: the first born from the dead (Revelation 1:5), the Highest of earthly kings (Revelation 1:5), Alpha and Omega (Revelation 1:8), the Living One (Revelation 1:18), Son of God (Revelation 2:18), and Faithful Witness (Revelation 3:14). If He can be all of these things to us, who then are you talking to and with whom are you walking? My life has presented for me various tasks, challenges, heartaches, pain, and suffering and at the same time presented many horrendous consequences from my own actions. How marvelous it is to know that Jesus died for us all. He suffered and died, yet He rose again three days later—full of power, love, and mercy.

The teachings of Jesus were not limited to a certain group of people or to one individual; but He taught all that would listen and follow Him. Although there may be times when we might find ourselves unable to physically be there in person to lend support to someone, prayer and biblical instruction can still be applied remotely. In a remote sense, you can offer support through such media as phone, email, or other available methods of communication. Communication of the gospel and the great teachings of Jesus Christ help to lead others, and it also keeps our focus on His love. Here's where we are trained and become true warriors and disciples for Christ. Moreover, the rewards are great for the recipient and the person providing the help. God provides each of us with gifts and talents, although they may only be seen visually when assisting and aiding someone else. We may not have the ability to recognize our own individual talents; and many times, others may be able to identify our gifts more quickly than we are able to perceive them ourselves. The possibility of this being my paradigm was the result of me ignoring the presence and significance of my gifts. My gifts were instilled in me and had to be awakened from the deepest sleep for the building of God's kingdom.

God provides us with gifts, talents, and the ability to help others for various reasons. As I struggled through many of my storms, I often felt like no one could help me through them. *Who cares?* I thought. The only thing that I could hear was, "Let her suffer." I closed my mind to the fact that someone somewhere could and would help me see the light I had been unaware of for so long. This is where and how I allowed my emotions to overshadow my view of reaching my destiny. But help was there—my help has been with me all the time. I am reminded of the hymnal "A Charge to Keep I Have" written by Charles Wesley. This song illustrates my commitment and willingness to be the called servant of God. I am fully committed to helping others as my Father provides for me each day. My charge to keep is the following declaration: "I, Patricia W. Goings take thee, Jesus, to be my father, my guide, and comforter, to have and to hold, from this day forward, for better or worse, for richer or poorer, in sickness and in health, to love and to cherish, forever and ever according to God's holy ordinance; and thereto I pledge thee my faith to you Lord God, I give myself to you to be used for your glory.

THE CALM DURING THE STORM

I've often found myself wanting something so much that nothing else seemed to matter. There were other times when I wanted to resolve things quickly, so I could move on, but sometimes it just did not work out that way. Patience, I had a hard time learning it. For several years of my life, patience just was not happening for me. However, what I did not realize in my early stages of life was that patience would have a significant role in my life. Trying to rush things just made it worse in many instances.

I remember my husband and me packing up our house to relocate to another area. The task of packing, in and of itself, was horrendous as there were boxes everywhere and so much to do. We found a home in a new development and were the first ones with a porch and a large, gated backyard. I was excited to relocate back into a city environment with street lights, movies, shopping malls, and restaurants everywhere. What appeared to be an exciting time suddenly transformed into a life-changing event. After all the packing was completed and the new residence was ready for move-in, moving day was closer now than in the previous months. Just when things seemed to be going well, all of a sudden something unfortunate happened. My husband had a heart

259

attack, which resulted in him having to have heart surgery. Suddenly, my life changed its course and direction. After much anticipation and now having to make medical decisions, the unpacking began as the choice to remain in our current residence was the favorable option. In that moment and for several days afterward, the hurt and disappointment faded. Renewing in my heart and mind what I had learned over the course of the many trials and struggles led me to pray and do it continuously. Reflecting back on Nehemiah's story, he realized the urgency of his situation and earnestly prayed that God would provide him with the help he needed. Nehemiah did not attempt to rebuild the gates without the help or guidance of the Lord.

> Lord, let your ear be attentive to the prayer of this your servant and to the prayer of your servants who delight in revering your name. Give your servant success today by granting him favor in the presence of this man."
> I was cupbearer to the king.
>
> NEHEMIAH 1:11 (NIV)

However, it was four months before Nehemiah was presented with an opportunity to make his request to the king (Nehemiah 2:1). Even while he was talking with the king, he silently prayed to God for favor (Nehemiah 2:4). Sometimes, there may be an interval of time before God answers our prayers, but we must learn to patiently wait until He does. Be that as it may, delay doesn't necessarily mean denial. Patience or long-suffering is a fruit of the Holy Spirit (Galatians 5:22), and there are rewards for those willing to put this character trait into practice. Nehemiah was a man of patience, and it is one of the reasons he is regarded as one of the greatest God-centered leaders of the Old Testament.

Nehemiah's patience was finally rewarded as the king consented to his request. Nehemiah was appointed governor of Judea; and along with a convoy, he was sent to his beloved city, Jerusalem. When he arrived, he worked tirelessly to rebuild the walls, and despite continual opposition (called "troublesome times" in Daniel 9:25), he miraculously completed the task in fifty-two days (Nehemiah 6:15-16). After remaining in Jerusalem for twelve years, Nehemiah was recalled to the Persian royal court. At the end of the book of Nehemiah, he makes this statement: "Remember me, O my God, for good" (Nehemiah 13:31). Patience teaches us to wait on God and wait knowing that in due course of our life's journey, our rewards will be joyous. These rewards are evident as according to the Beatitudes in the book of Matthew.

Seeing the crowds, He went up on the mountain; and when He was seated, His disciples came to Him. Then

He opened His mouth and taught them, saying: Blessed (happy, to be envied, and spiritually prosperous—with life-joy and satisfaction in God's favor and salvation, regardless of their outward conditions) are the poor in spirit (the humble, who rate themselves insignificant), for theirs is the kingdom of heaven! Blessed and enviably happy [with a happiness produced by the experience of God's favor and especially conditioned by the revelation of His matchless grace] are those who mourn, for they shall be comforted! Blessed (happy, blithesome, joyous, spiritually prosperous—with life-joy and satisfaction in God's favor and salvation, regardless of their outward conditions) are the meek (the mild, patient, long-suffering), for they shall inherit the earth! Blessed and fortunate and happy and spiritually prosperous (in that state in which the born-again child of God enjoys His favor and salvation) are those who hunger and thirst for righteousness (uprightness and right standing with God), for they shall be completely satisfied! Blessed (happy, to be envied, and spiritually prosperous—with life-joy and satisfaction in God's favor and salvation, regardless of their outward conditions) are the merciful, for they shall obtain mercy! Blessed (happy, enviably fortunate, and spiritually prosperous—possessing the happiness produced by the experience of God's favor and especially conditioned by the revelation of His grace, regardless of their outward conditions) are the pure in heart, for they shall see God! Blessed (enjoying enviable happiness, spiritually prosperous—with life-joy and satisfaction in God's favor and salvation, regardless of their outward conditions) are the makers and maintainers of peace, for they shall be called the sons of God! Blessed and happy and enviably fortunate and spiritually prosperous (in the state in which the born-again child of God enjoys and finds satisfaction in God's favor and salvation, regardless of his outward conditions) are those who are persecuted for righteousness' sake (for being and doing right), for theirs is the kingdom of heaven! Blessed (happy, to be envied, and spiritually prosperous—with life-joy and satisfaction in God's favor and salvation, regardless of your outward conditions) are you when people revile you and persecute you and say all kinds of evil things against you falsely on My account. Be glad and supremely joyful, for your reward in heaven is great (strong and intense), for in this same way people persecuted the prophets who were before you.

MATTHEW 5:1-12 (AMPC)

Exercising patience must be at the top of our list on a daily basis. Without it, we are often misunderstood, misrepresented, and will be treated unkindly in many instances. I have learned how to be patient, although at times it has been emotionally and physically challenging for me. I am happy that God has opened my eyes and my heart; and I am happy that I can now see His unconditional compassion for those who love Him and keep His commandments. Patience is a demonstration of walking by faith, hope, and God's love. In recent years I have come to realize that patience, commitment, and love are the keys to my life—love, most importantly, because of what our Father did when He sent Jesus to earth to die for us. Even though I struggled time after time throughout life, God always showed His patience and honored mine by always making a way when things seemed bleak.

This reminds me of a dream I had once. I did not understand the true meaning of the dream, nor did I understand what God was preparing me for. I dreamed that I was in the church, walking through and searching for help because I had been attacked by a large bird that appeared to be a pelican. I had scratches all over my back, but I was not afraid. I just needed someone to look at the wounds. As I entered the sanctuary, there stood several people in a group. One of them approached me and asked me if she could help. I told her what had happened, and she asked if she could see the wounds. As she viewed my back, she immediately beckoned for help. Due to the dreadful nature of the injury, the bystanders ascertained that the pastor needed to take a look at me. I was not bleeding in any way, but there were just scratches all over my back. As people began to draw closer to me, the pastor arrived and was astonished after seeing the carnage done to my back. The scratches on my back were so deep and ghastly that the onlookers mulled whether the bird had buried eggs within.

The revelation I received about this dream was that it was a time for preparation, as the adversary was about to attack me in a great way. However, I would not be fazed by his attack. The dream invoked in my mind a scripture quoted in the book of Isaiah.

> But he was pierced for our transgressions, he was crushed for our iniquities; the punishment that brought us peace was on him, and by his wounds we are healed.
>
> ISAIAH 53:5 (NIV)

By the stripes of Jesus I am made whole again. I have recovered from the sins and the past life that caused me to stray away from my destiny. Deliverance belongs to me now, and I can do all things through and in Christ.

> I rejoiced in the Lord greatly that now at length you have revived your concern for me. You were indeed concerned for me, but you had no opportunity. Not that I am speaking of being in need, for I have learned in whatever situation I am to be content. I know how to

be brought low, and I know how to abound. In any and every circumstance, I have learned the secret of facing plenty and hunger, abundance and need. I can do all things through him who strengthens me.

PHILIPPIANS 4:10-13 (ESV)

I now know the meaning of walking in faith, hope, and God's love. When going through appeared most difficult, unbeknownst to me I became stronger; for God was preparing me to do His will and lead others. Although the way and walk of life may get weary, I urge you to not dwell on the bad but go through by renewing your mind. We are created in the image of Christ, who is always with us. See yourself the way that God sees you— a victorious reflection of Himself! My goal and aim now are to continue loving the Lord with all that I am and be who He has ordained and appointed me to be. Psalm 34:19 decrees, "Many are the afflictions of the righteous: but the LORD delivereth him out of them all." No matter what you go through in life, know that God has called you to rise above it; and He's given you the will power to get through.

PRAYER

Most loving, heavenly Father, I thank you Lord for this day. I thank you for the many blessings that You have given me. I thank you for the blessings received and the ones that are destined for my future. I thank you for my family, friends, and most of all, Your love and kindness. I thank you, God, for allowing me to be used as a vehicle, ministering Your love, grace, and mercy to others. Thank you for granting me the gift to empower others through Your inspired words, telling the story of faith, hope, and Your love. I pray that hearts be touched and lives be changed for the glory of Your kingdom. Father, you know the struggle; and you know better than anyone else about the pain I have endured. I thank you, Lord, for seeing me through the hard times and the good times. Lord, I thank you! When I wanted to give up on myself, You impelled me to press on. When I wanted to surrender to the ills of the world, You sustained me with Your love and kindness. For this, I say thank you. So, Father, I ask now that you consecrate this book and let it empower and bless other women and children. I pray that the blood of Jesus will cover those that have read this book. I pray that You will pour out a fresh anointing of Your Holy Spirit upon me. I surrender now the words of this book, that they be glorified in Your kingdom. In the matchless name of Jesus I pray. Amen.

www.ingramcontent.com/pod-product-compliance
Lightning Source LLC
Chambersburg PA
CBHW021220090426
42740CB00006B/298